FEEDBACK MARKETING™

FEEDBACK MARKETING™

How to Duplicate Clients, Attract Prospects,
and Create Advocates... Without Talking

Dan Allison

Feedback
Marketing Group

Omaha Nebraska

Printed in the United States of America
on acid-free paper

FM

A WORD FROM THE AUTHOR

I want to thank you for taking your time to read through this book. The first sign that you are ready to take a different approach to the way that you improve and grow your business is your interest in reading this book. We have always been taught that you should listen twice as much as you talk. Rarely do we use that rule in business. Using the strategies in this book will allow you to do so. This will have a great impact on business.

This book will walk you step by step through using Feedback Marketing as a way to improve your relationships with your existing customers, gain more referrals for your business, and effectively approach the kinds of prospective clients that you truly want to reach. You will go through each step and learn how to conduct meaningful one-to-one interviews with your clients to uncover what they perceive your value to be. You will learn how to use focus groups to uncover why your clients behave the way that they do and to learn how they view your services. This is the first step to understanding how and why they refer people to your business. Most importantly, you will learn how to approach and involve your current clients in the growth of your business.

In addition to learning skills critical to improving your clients experience and learning how to gain more referrals from them, you will learn an unprecedented approach to gaining quality face time with the kinds of prospects you are targeting currently. The best part is that this approach allows you and a group of prospective clients to sit in a room with your guard down and have candid discussions about your value proposition, your services or products, and what you are trying to provide to individuals like them. You will learn what they value, what they don't, and what you can do to attract more clients like them. To add to those incredible benefits, you will earn new clients through meeting people in this setting.

We are in a time where people have lost trust and faith in the professionals that serve them. They don't believe the things that we say. That is because we talk too much and listen too little. Maybe it is time that we let them do the talking so that we can listen to the things that they need. The rest will take care of itself. I hope you enjoy this book and what it will teach you to do. If you implement just one of the three strategies detailed in this book, it will change the way you interact with clients and prospects. I hope that you find listening to your clients and prospects as beneficial as I have. They have all of the answers to the challenges that we all want to solve. We just need to ask them.

Respectfully,

Dan Allison
Founder
Feedback Marketing System

FM

CONTENTS

PREFACE

If you have made it this far, I will assume that you are the kind of professional that values not only your current clients, but also the future clients that you will serve. Now that we have come this far, let me ask you a question. What are the three things that make you and your service different than other individuals who do what you do for a living? I mean — three real things that you can list and say that you have, and they don't. Stop now, take some time to think, and write those three things down.

Let me ask you a second question. If I asked your best clients or your most valuable prospective clients to list the three things that separate you from other people who do what you do, what three things would they list? Would they list anything at all?

Somewhere along the line in many professional industries we have become obsessed with words like "value proposition" and "value added". We are fascinated by telling people that we provide a lot of value added service. The problem is — we don't really know if it is true. I know that may be difficult to hear, but it is true. Is your value proposition really valuable? Are your "value added" services really adding value? You don't know the answer to those questions and neither do I. The only people who can answer those questions honestly and objectively are our customers and prospects themselves. So, what do they say when you ask them? I understand that is why you are reading this.

My parents always told me that I have two ears and one mouth because I am supposed to listen twice as much as I talk. The sales managers that I have seen train would probably have you believe that you have eight mouths and no ears. After going from the mental health field to various industries in sales I was shocked to see how much presentation training or "sales" training people get. Almost none of these trainings taught people how to be straightforward, honest, ask questions, and listen. We have overcomplicated our most important industries. As a result, customers view service industries as selling industries.

As a consultant to companies throughout the country, I am frequently asked some of the following questions:

- How do I improve the retention of my top clients?
- How do I duplicate or get more referrals from my top clients?
- How can I close more prospective clients?
- How can we make our marketing more effective?

My initial answer to those questions sounds something like:

- What did your clients tell you when you asked about the retention issue?
- What did your clients say when you asked them how to effectively duplicate them?
- What did your prospects say when you ask them what is wrong with your value presentation?
- What did the people that you are targeting with your marketing say about how to make it more effective?

As you can image, people wonder initially why they are paying me. It is in our nature to want to be able to pay people to solve our problems. The reality is that no consultant can answer those questions for you. I don't care how clever their tag line is. Only the people that you are trying to serve can answer the questions that I have listed above. Have you asked them?

This book will address those issues and teach you step by step how to approach the people who have the answers to those questions. What you will find is that by implementing the strategies that are covered in the pages of this book, you will be able to accomplish many of your most challenging objectives. You will learn how to:

- Improve your client retention
- Gain more business from existing clients
- Enhance the experience of your existing clients

- Get more referrals from existing clients
- Gain face time with quality prospective clients in a non sales environment
- Convert prospects into advocates

How will you accomplish all these amazing feats? You are going to ask questions and you are going to listen! Revolutionary — I know. I am constantly accused of presenting the obvious. Why don't we do the obvious? Because we want to do it our own way and make everything harder than it needs to be. Well you can stop doing that today. You can learn from the mistakes that I have made. I have been part of building a company and selling it for millions only to turn around and build a company that lost millions. I learned an equal amount of valuable lessons from both. Oddly enough, I learned more from the loss than I did the gain.

So, before we get into the details and the three strategies that will help you accomplish the objectives that you have, I will regress a bit into my background and what lead me to become desperate enough to attempt these methods in my own business.

FM

ATTACK BY BATMAN AND THE DEADLY SHEEPDOG

I had never felt like a salesman before. There was a time in the mental health field where people called me things like Golden Boy and The Chosen One. So why did I find myself being accosted by a sheep dog in some woman's kitchen while her four-year-old boy attacked me with the loudest cap gun that I had ever heard on a Friday night? We had to make a sale, that's how.

My background is in Special Education and Psychology. I have always had a fascination with why people do the things that they do. From misbehavior to success, I always wondered why and how. This passion led me to gain formal education degrees in those fields. While in school I began to work with a non-profit mental health company. I was very fortunate to have been given the title of Chief Operating Officer at the age of 23. This was a big responsibility as we had hundreds of employees and brought in tens of millions of dollars annually.

After being involved in that field for a while, two partners and I began our own for-profit mental health company. Three years after starting the company and experiencing incredible growth, we received an offer to sell the company for millions of dollars. We were ready to sell and the offer was good. My mental health career was over almost before it began. After agreeing to a non-compete clause I realized that I had essentially signed away my ability to do the only thing that I was qualified to do for a reasonable amount of money. I was far from retiring on the beach and doing the Macarena all day. I needed to be productive.

1

In my youthful idiocy I quickly assumed that any business I would be involved with would turn into gold. I was quick to invest and play an active role in a variety of companies in the banking, finance, real estate and insurance and investment fields.

I thought that all of these fields provided a valuable service. I thought that all of the professionals who worked in these fields showed up to work at 8 a.m. with people waiting in the parking lots for them to open so that they could come in and buy stuff. I did not understand that you had to prospect for new business. I had never even heard that word.

I knew very quickly that if I were going to be successful, I would need to learn how to "sell" like everyone told me that you had to. I spent time with the investment and insurance professionals in workshops and seminars, I watched as realtors provided services to clients for months only to have them move to another realtor and sell a week later. I even saw investment advisors explain 30% losses to their clients and then say "keep me in mind if your friends or family need any help."

The night that changed everything for me was the night that a young salesman asked me to attend an appointment with him so that I could "learn." He explained to me that this was different from my other experiences because this was an in house sales appointment. In the mental health field, in house had a very different meaning.

I agreed that we would go and was excited because the young man told me that he was going to present strategies that would change the woman's life. I was about to witness something amazing. I want to walk you through my one and only in house sales experience:

Upon the door opening I noticed the welcoming aroma of some Italian dish. What I didn't realize is that it wasn't just an aroma; they were actually eating during the appointment. As we sat down to begin changing the woman's life we were in slight competition with cartoons on the nearby television, set at high volume.

Ignoring the distractions and confident in our ability to overcome the "mild" challenges, the young man began speaking confidently. After all, he was going to change her life and he had the glossy brochures and charts and graphs to prove it. You can imagine my surprise when he and I found ourselves looking at one another as she casually talked on the phone for the third time in twenty minutes. You see, she was expecting an incredibly important phone call. Our life changing charts and graphs would have to wait.

As the ultimate professional got into the heart of the chart or graph, I was awakened by the cracking BANG of a cap gun held by her young boy named Jimmy. Jimmy was four years old. He wore a Batman mask, a Batman cape, and Batman underwear. Thank God that he had the courtesy to put on the underwear. Jimmy thought that it was funny to place the metal cap gun with the long red tape sticking out of it behind my head and bang the thing every few minutes. I don't recall whether my prevailing thought was that they still made those kinds of cap guns or that the sparks that shot out as a result of said BANG may ignite the Aqua Net hairspray in my hair.

Temporarily distracted from the life changing presentation I regained my focus although never my dignity. As we wrapped the successful appointment I remember the noise that changed my life. I heard the slight jingle of chain approaching from behind me. It sounded like a delightful little pet.

Instead, I met face to face with a 105-pound sheep dog named Barney. Barney and I had an instant connection. So much so that he decided to go under the kitchen table and gently place his face where babies are made. When I say place his face, I mean more that he began to attack me as though I had smuggled several large T-bones into my pants.

Stunned at the act, I briefly attempted to stop Barney with a gentle eye poke. Barney however mistook the gesture for a request to be more aggressive. It was at that point I realized that my only option was to let Barney "finish."

It was when the mild asthma attack began that the woman told us that she "appreciated" our time and that she would definitely be in touch. We had changed her life you see, and that is what people do after you change their life. They wait for some time and then get in touch. She never got in touch.

This final trauma was all I needed to realize that I was not cut out for prospecting in any way shape or form. For my life I could not understand why people were not lined up outside of the doors of the different professionals in our companies. We had things that they needed. We were the ultimate professionals. We could change their life! Why weren't they lined up outside of my door?

I will credit my wife with a simple answer to a very simple question. The question was, "Why won't more people take advantage of what we have to offer and why don't clients refer us?" The answer was quite simple, "Why don't you ask them?"

You see, my wife is not a high level business coach. She is not a motivational speaker who will teach you about success and giving people what they want. She doesn't even teach Fortune 500 companies to seize opportunity and the moment. She was a wonderful stay at home mother who had simplified all of the industry's challenges with one response to my question. Why don't I ask them?

My quest began to find the answers to all of my questions. I was revitalized with enthusiasm as I began to fall back into the skill set that made me successful in the mental health field. I would talk less and listen more. I would ask people directly what they found valuable, what they didn't find valuable, and where our services fell in between. I began what has now become Feedback Marketing.

My first objective was to find a way to learn what we had to do to get our current clients to be raving fans of our business and refer us to more people like them. These people had entrusted us with services and areas of their lives that were important to them. Surely, they weren't unhappy with the services that we were providing. I wanted to recruit some help from our existing client base to solve my challenges.

The first thing I did was sit down with a list of our existing clients. At the time, we had a couple hundred what you would call "A" clients. By that I simply mean they are the kinds of clients who were very profitable for our company and those with whom we had seemingly had good relationships. I identified a group of 50 of the most influential clients and decided that I would conduct five focus groups. While we will get into detail about how to do this, focus groups are essentially small groups of like-minded people who come together to hear a presentation and take part in solving a problem.

What happened during these focus groups was amazing. The clients were flattered that they were selected as respected relationships and were very eager to help a company they trusted. I was able to be straightforward with them because of the focus group setting and talk to them about the challenges we were facing. I began the focus group by outlining what services we were trying to expand and what kind of customers we were trying to attract. After doing so, I asked them questions about what they saw our primary value to be. I asked them what areas we could focus on to improve their experience. I even asked them how we should approach our current client base about referrals in the most appropriate way.

Those five focus groups alone lead to more feedback than 1,000 surveys could have provided. The clients genuinely appreciated that I let them into the business side of our operations and respected them enough to ask for their opinion. The referral opportunities that arose through the referral discussion were completely unexpected. Our current clients made offers for us to come in and address their employees, friends, and other associations to help in our effort to grow our business. It was as though they had only seen us as having individual relationships; now they understood the business aspect. It was incredible. Those who did not participate in a focus group came in for one-to-one meetings. I simply called them and told them that we were looking at expanding our services and as we did, we wanted some advice and guidance from some of our most respected relationships. They came in for an hour or more and sat one-to-one with only one intention; to talk about our business. This was the first time we had actually asked our clients to consider being a source of feedback. The one-to-one sessions were a mirror image of the focus groups. We talked about our business and what areas we were trying to expand. We talked about our current clients and the kinds of clients we were trying to attract. We got feedback on what we do well and what could be improved. Finally, we approached the topic of referrals and how to most comfortably ask for them. I had never felt comfortable saying "who do you know that needs my service." I did want to make sure that my clients understood that, but we still wanted to grow with the right people. These sessions were amazing for our relationships and our business.

While making great headway into the issues with our current clients, I decided to try something that nobody had ever tried in our entire organization. We had hundreds of employees, millions in revenues, hundreds of thousands of potential prospects in our market; we had never engaged in one focus group. I had a large list of potential customers that we had contacted by E-mail, direct-mail marketing, and in general continued to send things they obviously didn't care about. I simply wanted to know what they found valuable about our offering, how we could improve it, and how to truly bring value to people like them.

I called people on the list and was very straightforward. I explained that we owned a financial services company and were looking to understand our target customer better. I offered a small $50 gift card for them to participate in a small focus group. Within one hour of calling, I had ten participants. What was also nice was that I qualified them on the phone to make sure they were the right kind of client to give us feedback. If someone would ask me if I wanted to run an advertisement for $500 that would guarantee me face time with 10 qualified prospects, I would tell them every day and twice on Sundays. It was simply that. I only paid people who agreed to participate. It didn't cost me money until they were in front of me.

When they arrived, I simply explained that we spend our resources marketing our "value" to them, but we had never really sat with them and discussed the value in an effort to learn from them. I spent the first half presenting what we did and what we had that we thought was valuable. I spent the second half of the group asking what they found valuable, what we were missing, and how we could be more valuable to people like them. I had never seen an environment like this. Ten completely engaged prospects at my office on my time without a sheep dog in site.

I learned a great deal from that series of groups, changed a lot about the way we communicated our services, and to top it off;

many of them approached me to discuss their challenges. I actually gained clients nearly every time I did a focus group. I cared enough to listen. That is the kind of professional people are attracted to. I knew that if I presented our value to 50 people in five focus groups and none of them became clients, I would have 50 questionnaires and five hours of feedback to tell me why. I could not lose.

I have been able to help thousands of professionals across the country implement these three simple strategies into their business. From large charities and churches wanting to better understand their donors, to small financial firms trying to be more valuable to business owners. These strategies are some of the best marketing dollars that you could ever spend. These strategies allow you to market your services to your ideal clients and prospects in a non-selling environment and have them tell you how to approach them. The combination of these strategies is a new kind of marketing that I call, Feedback Marketing.

FM

WHY DOES
FEEDBACK MARKETING WORK?

Feedback Marketing is the combination of two simple concepts. You will hear in any business circle that people work "on their business" or "in their business." What that means is that if you are working "on your business" you are doing the planning, the marketing, and the high-level critical thinking. If you are working "in your business" you are engaged in providing service and actively prospecting new clients.

Feedback Marketing will allow you to work on your business and in your business simultaneously. It will let you present your services, talk about your business plans and growth goals, and market your value while gaining feedback from the people who have the power to help you grow your business. Imagine for a moment that you have ten participants come into a workshop or a seminar to learn about your services. You have the environment perfect, you have a great meal planned, you are a skilled presenter, and tonight is the night you will gain more clients. You give your skilled presentation, everyone loves you and your food, they all tell you they will be in touch, and then you call them relentlessly to "follow up."

What went wrong with the presentation? That is a million dollar question. The problem is that they have the answer. What if those same people came into the room without the fancy dinner, listened intently to the presentation and took notes, and then told you why they would or would not use the service? Would that be valuable? That is Feedback Marketing. It allows you to present your value to any population that you want to in an open and honest environment. Rather than simply talking, it allows you to spend more time

8

listening to what their needs are and whether what you talked about meets their needs. When it does, they give you great feedback and take the next steps to using the service. When it does not, they tell you what's broken so that you can fix it. This book will show you how to do that.

The key to implementing this system is to change the way your clients and prospective clients view you. They cannot see you as a wholesaler, or sales person, or service manager. They need to see you as a business person and understand your business objectives. When they understand that, they are able to give you guidance and advice on how to accomplish your objectives. If you have something that they need, they will naturally use what you have. At the same time they can also help you learn and become advocates of your service. All you have to do is ask.

Consulting is a multi-billion dollar industry. People hire professionals like me to solve their problems. This approach will allow you to hire the real experts to solve your problems; your clients and prospects. They are the real consultants you should be using. There is a silver bullet for growing a business. What we all have to realize is that our clients and prospective clients hold the silver bullet. This book will teach you how to ask them for it respectfully and then ask them how they would like you to use it.

FM

THE THREE
FEEDBACK MARKETING STRATEGIES

There are three basic strategies that this book will walk you through step by step. Each on its own will have a dramatic impact on your business. Used together and consistently, your entire approach to marketing and the way you acquire clients will transform.

I had a client who was invited every year to attend a golf outing in Scottsdale, Arizona. This was a great trip because it was hosted by his top client. This client was a very wealthy executive with Boeing. This wealthy client every year would bring about 10 other high level executives and his friend who was also his financial advisor. Previously, these trips had not yielded much business for the financial advisor. While these people were the ideal fit for his business, approaching them and giving them business cards did not work. He tried to give his "30 second elevator speech" to talk about why he was different, but it seemed to fall short of what they were looking for.

After being trained in Feedback Marketing, he attended this trip with a new group of executives. He refrained from throwing business cards around and rather listened to where the conversation went. It inevitably went to the economy and the downturn that it had taken. He listened as one executive talked about what the down turn had done to his portfolio and the trust that he had lost in his advisor. Rather than pounce, the advisor continued to listen as others jumped in and agreed. To this point, they did not know what the advisor did for a living. The advisor began to ask the others what their experience had been like in the economy. They talked about their challenges and their struggles and how they wish someone would just shoot them straight.

He questioned and peopled talked and he realized that he had conducted an impromptu focus group. He listened the entire time and did not talk. At the end of the discussion, one of the guys asked, "So what end of the aviation business are you in." To which he replied, "I am actually not in the aviation industry at all." When they said, "So what do you actually do for a living?" He said, "I provide second opinions and investment analysis for aviation executives." They drew straws the next day to see who got to ride in the golf cart with him. This is the power of listening and feedback.

INTEREACTIVE CLIENT SURVEYS

The first strategy that will be detailed in the coming section is what I call Interactive Client Surveys. They are one-to-one interviews with your top clients that will accomplish many objectives. They will allow you to gain valuable feedback from your clients on your service, any area that you could improve to help them more, and will tell you how to approach that client about referrals. Most of the time, they will inadvertently lead to more referrals.

Why Interactive Client Surveys? Unless you are in the car business or the restaurant business most high level customers find mailed surveys insulting. Think about the message that those surveys send. You are special to us. So special in fact that we sent out this bulk mailing and asked every customer the exact same questions that we asked you. Even though we have done a million dollars of business with you, your college kid got the same survey. Oh, and because we did bulk mail we saved on postage!

Is that really the message to send to the clients who are so important to you? This first strategy will solve that problem and yield the absolute opposite result. Not only will you receive your top clients' time, get valuable feedback, learn how to get more referrals, and learn how to insure that they stay with you; but they will thank you for taking the time to do so. People like to know that they are important. They like to feel as though they were selected from a crowd and that their opinions matter. This is a very powerful strategy that everyone who values their clients should implement.

We will walk through this process from beginning to end.

CLIENT CENTERED FOCUS GROUPS

As an alternative to a one-to-one setting, client focus groups are very efficient and powerful. These groups allow you to bring in 8-10 of your most valuable relationships and conduct a discussion session. Many organizations worry about their customer base giving negative feedback. There are two things that I tell those organizations. Number one is that focus groups aren't supposed to simply be a format to hear that you are the most wonderful company that your clients are never going to refer anyone to. You are supposed to get some criticism so that you can improve. Secondly, these groups allow clients to vent and probably saved them as a customer. They will appreciate that you took the time to listen.

The groups are a great way to learn from current clients what they value, how to improve, get their feedback on a new product or service that you are rolling out to your clients base; or simply to learn how to differentiate yourself from the competition. When executed every couple of months, focus groups are one the least expensive and most enjoyable events you will do as an organization. We will walk step by step through how to conduct these groups.

PROSPECT CENTERED FOCUS GROUPS

Think of the hours and days that you have spent in brainstorming meetings, marketing meetings, trainings and the like trying to develop additional value for prospective clients. You designed the value added, you talked about how you're going to market the value added, and then you talk about how crazy your prospects will go over the value add. Only to find that the response was not what you thought it would be.

Think about how powerful it is to know that any time you have something that you think your prospects will respond to, you will have a way to either confirm that thought and gain new clients while doing so, or learn that you are the one who is crazy and you need to go back to the drawing board. Knowing how to do prospect focus groups will not just save you thousands and thousands of dollars in future wasted marketing money, they will save your sanity.

Learning how to conduct prospect focus groups will give you a tool that you can use any time you want to sit with a group of prospects and present an idea or product to them. You can hire a consultant for $40,000 to come in and help you design your product, your marketing plan, the direct mail pieces, and at the end of the day, get no response. Focus groups would have solved that before you spent the money.

The prospect focus group is a commonly used technique; however, it is normally reserved only for the multi-billion dollar fortune 500 company who hires over-paid research firms to tell them that blue is better than red. This section of the book will teach you what the large market research firms don't want you to know. You can do that research without them. We will walk step by step through the process of conducting small focus groups with qualified prospects as a means of marketing your value, and learning how to approach the people with whom you want to grow your business.

FM

INTERACTIVE CLIENT SURVEYS

Turning Passive Clients into Active Advocates and Developing Bullet-Proof Retention

YOU WILL GAIN

- Valuable feedback on how to improve areas that can be improved
- Feedback on what your clients see as your most valuable service or product
- A client with a clear idea of your business objectives and your ideal prospects
- A client who understands their role in helping you achieve those objectives
- Improved retention through listening to the clients' real needs
- More referrals from existing valuable clients
- A stronger relationship with existing valuable clients

INTERACTIVE CLIENT SURVEYS

I met a mortgage banker in Florida who had built a very solid business. He did well during the real estate boom and was smart enough not to live a lifestyle accordingly. When we began our discussions together, he told me that his business was going well, his marketing efforts had paid off and that loans were consistently coming through the door. He said the problem with his business was that his referrals were "broken." When I asked what he meant he went on to explain that he was averaging about 20 referrals per month. Now, for a loan officer, that is a big number and would not seem to be something that is "broken." He went on to explain that of the 20 referrals, 18 of them (on average) were people with severely impaired credit and income issues. And, after working for hours on each loan, many did not close. The ones that did were not profitable for the time he spent. He was consistently being referred the kind of client that he did not want to build his business serving.

When we went deeper into the problem he explained that he had given a presentation to the Realtor Association about creative ways to help people who have impaired credit. Little did he understand that he would become the impaired credit expert. Realtors were looking for a good resource primarily because nobody wanted to spend all the time to solve those problems. While he had established solid relationships with his referral sources, they were going to bankrupt him.

When we began to discuss who he wanted to focus his services on he went on to show me a business plan, his goals, his objectives and how his 15 years in the business had qualified him to work with a high level business owner who had complicated income issues however could easily afford a big home. He had certifications and licenses that allowed him to do so but he continued to get the referrals that were holding him back. When I asked why Realtors were still sending him bankrupt clients when he clearly had a business plan designed to help a different population he said the answer that I hear from many business professionals. They have never really seen my business plan.

Why is it that we spend time and work so hard on our goals and objectives and what kinds of clients will get us there but we fail to tell those who matter most about them? Our top clients, our referrals sources, and all the people who day in and day out are out meeting the kinds of people that we want to meet don't know what our plans are and who we want to grow our business with.

This mortgage banker scheduled 5 one-to-one meetings with Realtors who had been great referral sources for him. He brought them into his office by asking if they would come in and give him some feedback on his business because he respected them. He presented his business model and the direction he wants to go with it. He talked about the ideal client he is going to focus on and why that is his ideal client. After presenting this plan he asked the Realtor one question, "If you were in my position, how would you approach

Realtors of your caliber with this plan." The Realtor said that to start, he needed to come back and present to the same group on high level financing and how it works to begin to be known as a specialist in that rather than impaired credit. She told him that she did not know that he was focusing on a different population and about all the clients in the last year she could have sent him. She thought he wanted to do impaired credit. The mortgage banker walked out of his first Interactive Client Survey with an invitation to come speak to 60 Realtors about high level financing, a stronger relationship with a valuable referral source, and a loan that made him $14,000 in commission that the Realtor had been working on.

Sometimes we get so wrapped up in serving our clients that we don't take the time to think about whether or not our clients and referrals sources really understand the business side of our business. They think of us as individuals who solved a specific need that they had but fail to see the business side of what we do. Therefore, they are not the best advocates for our services. Many times, we have an army of people who like us and trust us wondering around as huge opportunity walks right in front of them.

I want you to do an exercise. Write down what your goals and objectives are for bringing on new clients in the coming year. How many clients would you like to add to your business, what are the key characteristics of the kinds of clients that you want to add, and what services do you feel are most valuable to them? To review, how many clients do you want to add, what characteristics do you want them to have, and what service do you want to provide to them?

Now I would ask, if I asked your most valuable clients and referral relationships how many clients you were taking on next year, what kind of clients you would be working with, and what services that you want to focus on; could they answer any of those three questions? Chances are that they would not know how to answer those questions. Our clients typically see us as a relationship, not a business. Therefore, they don't understand the strategy behind what we are doing. People that we would love to meet walk by our clients and referral partners all day long without being stopped because we do a poor job of letting them in on the business. Imagine how many clients approached their Realtors and said, "I want to buy the million dollar home, but as a business owner, my income is complicated. Do

16

you know anyone who works with that?" The Realtors thought, not really, but I do have an impaired credit expert who works in the $70,000 range. We need to give them the right tools, and the right description of the clients we want to serve.

We have to spend the time to work one-to-one with our most trusted relationships and share with them our business objectives. Not simply to share the objectives with them, but to gain advice about how they would approach the objectives. You have some very influential and intelligent people within your client base who can offer incredible advice and resources. Chances are that your client interaction is limited to lunches or meetings where the focus is on them. At best you may throw in at the end "Keep me in mind if you run into anyone who needs my service." You mean someone with impaired credit? Will do!

I ask people who their employer is nearly every time I meet them. When they are employees, they tell me the name of their large company. When they are self employed, they go on about how they work for themselves. I disagree on both accounts. Your employer is your client base. In both of these scenarios that I just described — if you don't have clients, you don't have income.

Think about your top clients and your top referral relationships for a moment like you would an employer. What do you do every year without exception with your employer? You have an annual review. The focus is on you and your business. You talk about the objectives that you had for the year and what you accomplished and you talk about the goals and objectives that you have for next year. Then, the boss gives you feedback on your plan and any advice that they can. They also offer assistance in accomplishing your plan. Your clients and referral partners are no different. They will gladly talk to you about your goals and objectives and give you input into how best to approach those goals. They will also offer assistance where they can. Do you have a method of sitting one-to-one with your most influential clients in an environment with no interruptions to discuss this most important matter?

Interactive Client Surveys are a very strategic approach to meeting one-to-one with those who matter the most to your business and can have the most influence on your business. Instead of talking about golf and the weather, you have an actual agenda and accomplish a great deal. You will be able to talk about your goals, your challenges, and then gain their valuable insight. Real client relationships deserve more than a bulk mail survey. The results of each one of these one-to-one meetings will be:

- Valuable feedback on the experience your clients have
- Valuable feedback on how to improve areas that can be improved
- A client with a clear idea of your business objectives and your ideal prospects
- A client who understands their role in helping you achieve those objectives
- Improved retention through listening to the clients real needs
- More referrals from being top of mind with the client
- A stronger relationship with existing valuable clients

Those are a lot of great benefits for taking an hour out of your life to talk to your clients. Imagine the impact of having one Interactive Client Survey per week over the course of the year. You will spend 50 hours this year in meaningful, enjoyable conversation with your most valuable relationships talking about your business, your growth objectives and gain their advice. Do you think this could have an impact on your business?

If there is one of the three strategies covered in this book that I feel is a must for any professional or organization that values their clients, it is this one. This will be the best time that you invest in your business. You will see that all you need to do is develop your process and then implement it. The time you spend up front should be minimal. We will walk through this process step by step.

Step 1- Identify What Your Challenges Are

The first step to implement Interactive Client Surveys in your business is to write down clearly what you feel your challenges are in your business and why you feel that they may be challenges. Do you struggle to get referrals from your clients? Do you feel that they may not really understand your service or who you want to work with? Are you struggling with client retention?

Whatever you feel your primary challenges are, you should write them down. Now, I know when I read books and the author tells me to stop and do something, many times I read on. I am encouraging you that prior to implementing this process, you follow these steps exactly. Writing down your challenges will outline what you are trying to overcome through implementing Interactive Client Surveys. It will be the blueprint of your meetings. You need to have a measuring stick and clear cut challenges that you need to overcome. If you do not have clear objectives, you will find that these meetings will slowly digress into talks about family and golf. There is another time for that. I have written an example from one of my clients below to give you an idea of how to write your challenges:

EXAMPLE

The primary challenges that I face in my day to day business that stop me from achieving the level of success that I would like to are:

1. *I spend too much time performing low payoff activities to serve clients that I should not have chosen to serve in the first place.*

2. *I am taking clients that I should not serve because I am not getting enough quality referrals from my clients and other professional relationships that I have spent time building.*

3. *I feel as though some of my key clients may not be as happy as they can be with my service although I don't know what exactly I can do to improve our relationship.*

4. *I feel like I am taking a reactive approach to my business and don't have a real proactive plan to market my business and obtain referrals.*

Do you see how all of these things are inter-related and how one impacts the other? Not getting enough quality referral clients leads to serving lower payoff clients. Doing lower payoff activities can impact the service levels of your top clients and may result in unhappy clients. Not doing anything about it will result in all of the challenges worsening. You must have a proactive and consistent approach to resolving these issues. The common theme in the example above is that if top clients would refer more quality business, the others would resolve themselves. Therefore, top clients are the ones who can help solve the challenges. Now we know why we need to hold one-to-one meetings with top clients. We have identified what challenges we are trying to solve that will have a bottom line impact on our relationships and our business.

Step 2 – Write Your Purpose Statement and Objectives

After you have developed a complete list of the challenges that you face, the next step is to write what I call a Purpose Statement and clearly define the objectives that you have for conducting the one-to-one meetings. These should be very clearly defined objectives and will be the basis for many of the things we will talk about in the coming pages. Writing a good Purpose Statement will be the foundation for how you explain to your clients what you are trying to accomplish when you invite them to spend some time with you. Your objectives will help you shape the questions that you will ask the clients for feedback on.

In general, you're Purpose Statement and objectives will be your measuring stick. You will look back after concluding you're first ten Interactive Client Surveys and look at your Purpose Statement to determine how successful you have been.

The best way to begin your list of objectives is to consider that there are no barriers to what you can accomplish through meeting with your top clients or referral partners. That anything that you want to occur will occur. You will see that there are really two main components of your objectives. There will be the objectives that detail the things that you want to insure that you share with your client and that they walk out of the meeting clearly understanding, and there will be the things that you want to learn from your clients and the things that you want to walk out of the meeting understanding.

So think about it, what do your clients or referral partners not clearly understand today about your business model, your services, your growth plan, your objectives for the future, or anything that you feel they should firmly understand? You will have the opportunity at the beginning of the meeting to share those things with the client. These are the things that you will be asking the client for feedback on. You will be asking how best to accomplish the objectives, or explain the service, or approach your target market. Begin now, by writing down some of the things that you would like your client to better understand. You can use the example below for a template.

Secondly, you need to complete a list of the things that you want to learn from your clients as part of this process. Again, don't worry about how you word them because these are your objectives and your clients will not see them. They will simply help you structure the meeting. If you could ask your client to help you with any area of your business, what areas do you feel they could really have an impact on? The following is an example of a Purpose Statement and clearly defined objectives:

I want to conduct one-to-one Interactive Client Surveys because I feel that I have taken a reactive approach to growing my business. I feel that through conducting some one on one meetings with my most valuable relationships I can overcome some of the primary challenges that I face in my business and develop a more proactive and effective way to build my business. The primary objectives for the initial Interactive Client Surveys will be:

WHAT I WANT TO SHARE WITH MY CLIENTS:

- *To clearly outline for my clients the focus of my business and what services that I really want to expand on.*

- *To clearly define for my clients the characteristics of our ideal client and why we want to focus our growth on that population.*

- *To discuss a few changes that I am considering implementing in my business.*

21

WHAT I WANT FROM MY CLIENTS:

- *To receive feedback on the current service levels my clients experience and understand what they feel is most valuable about their experience with us.*

- *To receive feedback on any areas that we may be able to improve on to become more referable.*

- *To gain our top client's insight into our future objectives and what advice they would have for where we will focus our efforts.*

- *To learn how our clients believe they can contribute to our growth plan and learn how they want to be involved in our growth.*

- *To get feedback on some of the changes that I plan to make in the coming year to the way that we provide service.*

Do you see how these objectives are two-fold? I want to insure that my clients leave with a very clear vision of my business model, the kinds of clients that are important to us, and what role our top clients can have in helping us (MARKETING). But, I also want to gain their feedback and insight on the goals that I have (FEEDBACK). You will see in the coming steps that these objectives will form what I present to my clients when they come in and the questions that I ask them to discuss.

Again, do not take short cuts when you are developing this process. You will spend only a few hours developing this entire process and the impact will be significant. If you don't take the time to write each step down, you will look back on your meetings and realize that they did not accomplish your objectives because you did not clearly identify them. At the end of this section, you will see a complete example of a complete outline from the Challenges to the Questionnaire. Each step is important to have down in writing.

By the end of the second step, you should have clearly outlined what your challenges are and what you would like to enlist your clients help in overcoming. You should have a clearly define Purpose

Statement and clearly outlined objectives. Once you have completed these steps, you should move on to selecting which clients and referral relationships you would like to include in this process.

Step 3 – Selecting Your Clients

Now that you know what challenges you want to focus on overcoming and what you want to accomplish, you have to decide which relationships you want to enlist to get feedback from. These relationships will mainly be current clients but you may also want to bring in some influential referral relationships. I encourage most of the organizations that I work with to do one exercise called the Rule of 100 to help them with this selection process.

The first thing that I would recommend that you do is print out a list of all of the client and referral relationships that you currently have. One by one, walk through your list and ask yourself one question; "If I had 100 of these relationships, what would my business look like?" If that question brings a smile to your face, put them on your invite list. They are more than likely either someone that you really enjoy serving or someone who has been very good to your business. They may simply be someone who has significant influence over the kinds of people that you would like to focus on for the growth of your business.

If you don't get those kinds of feelings when you look at the relationships name, they are more than likely someone that you don't enjoy serving. They may not be profitable for you -- they may simply be rude people. You have got to begin a proactive approach to growing specifically with the kinds of people that you enjoy working with. That does not mean that the service of the people who don't make the list should suffer. They simply don't need to be a focus of your growth effort and certainly don't need to be part of your Interactive Client Survey process.

Don't get fixated on how many of these quality relationships you have. Don't compromise quality for quantity. You will simply be wasting your time meeting with people that you don't want to duplicate. Sometimes you will look at the list that you have compiled to participate in your Interactive Client Surveys and realize that there are some names on the list that make you nervous. This is because you probably have not exceeded their service expectations and you know it. This will be your opportunity to deal with that issue head on and acknowledge that fact. You will gain incredible respect from these clients for having the courage to deal with your service issues head on. Chances are, you will retain a client, remind them why they decided to do business with you in the first place, and take them from someone who is never likely to refer to someone who is likely to refer in the future.

Ideally after completing this exercise you have come up with 40-50 clients and referral relationships to meet with. While you can have as many of these appointments per week as you want, I recommend just doing one a week as a consistent part of your marketing and expansion efforts. This will insure that the meetings never become overwhelming and that you give the follow up the attention that it deserves.

At this point, you should have clearly defined your challenges and have your Purpose Statement and objectives outlined. You should also have your list of qualified clients and referral relationships ready to go. Now you need to put some structure to the actual meeting to insure that you have clear guidelines to follow when your clients and referral relationships give you the time.

Step 4 – Structuring the Meeting

As I mentioned earlier in the book, this is not a meeting to discuss current events and simply catch up on things. This is a business meeting with well defined objectives and goals and should have an equally structured and well defined agenda. As you will see, the structure for your Interactive Client Surveys will be identical to the structure that you will set up for your client and prospect focus groups. You will need to develop an Introduction, a Presentation, Discussion Questions, and a Questionnaire. The four sections should be written so that you have a clear idea of how long each will take and what you plan to say. Again, you have to plan for this. Once the development work is done, you can implement it and duplicate it. Anything worth doing takes some time and thought to develop well. The first component of the meeting will be the Introduction.

Introduction

The Introduction will be a critical piece of your meeting. It is the first five minutes when you and your client sit down and you lay out why you have asked them to spend their time with you. Again, it is critical that your client understand that this is not just a meeting to catch up and chat. You need to take control of the meeting to let them know why you have asked them to come in today, what you hope to accomplish, and what exactly will occur over the hour of time you have asked of them. I break the Introduction into three main categories:

Why Did I Decide to Conduct These Interactive Client Surveys?

The first thing that your client or referral relationship needs to understand is why you decided to conduct some client surveys in the first place. This should be a summary of what your challenges are and what the client has to do with helping solve those challenges. This is where you are letting your client behind the curtain of your business. Don't worry about exposing yourself and letting your client see that you have challenges, everyone does. They will respect you for talking directly to them about it. The first part of your Introduction may sound something like:

> *John, I want to thank you for taking your time to come in and talk to me today. I want to begin by talking to you a little bit about what led me to conduct some of these meetings with my clients, what I hope to accomplish by doing so, and let you know exactly what to expect out of the time that I have asked of you.*
>
> *As you know, I have been in business now for just over ten years. I have been very blessed to continue to build my business with many quality clients. When I look forward at the next ten years, I want to insure that I use what I have learned to continue to grow the business with the right kinds of clients. When I really think about the kinds of clients that we want to do business with, there are some characteristics*

that really jump out at me. I realize that we do business with a lot of different people, but, there are those select clients that just really seem to be a good fit for our business. Rather than continue on the path we have, I wanted to really focus on what our most respected clients value in our service, how we can improve the service, and on growing with the right kinds of clients.

I decided, a good first step would be to clearly identify out of my 200 clients, which ones that I really enjoy serving and which ones that I would really love to duplicate. This was a small portion of my client base. You are one of those clients. I wanted to get each of them to come in one-to-one and have a different kind of conversation than we usually do. I wanted to make sure that my top clients have a good feel for my vision for the company. I want to insure that my top clients understand what services we want to focus on and what kind of clients we want to grow the company with. Finally, and most importantly, I wanted to gain the insight my top clients can share on our value, areas we can improve, and their guidance on how to accomplish the growth that we want to accomplish.

By saying something like the script above, your client will have a good foundation for why you have decided to ask for their time. They will be flattered that out of all of your clients, they are someone that you respect enough to seek advice from them. They will also understand that you are looking toward the future and looking at growing your company with some select clients. Finally, they will understand that their feedback will be very helpful in accomplishing that overall objective. That brings us to the second part of the Introduction. After explaining why you decided to bring them in to the meeting, you have to walk them through what you want to accomplish.

What Do I Want to Accomplish By Doing These Meetings?

After explaining to your client what challenges you are facing and why you were compelled to put together some of these one-to-one meetings, it is important for them to understand what the objectives are for the meeting and what you hope to accomplish. While you can be vague and just tell your clients you want to use the feedback to be better at what you do and the service they receive, I recommend a more formal explanation. This piece of the Introduction may sound like this:

As I mentioned, I realize that some of my top clients may not have a good feel for the vision of our company and where we want to take it in the future. This is obviously a big oversight on our part. We have a lot of talented clients and not having them involved in our business objectives is not a smart decision. I want to insure that through these meetings, our clients gain perspective about what we are trying to build and why. I also want to get feedback on certain issues. At this point, I want to walk you through the objectives that I outlined for these meetings. The primary goals and objectives for the meeting are:

WHAT I WANT TO SHARE WITH MY CLIENTS:

- *To clearly outline for my clients the focus of my business and what services that I really want to expand on.*

- *To clearly define for my clients the characteristics of our ideal client and why we want to focus our growth on that population.*

- *To discuss a few changes that I am considering implementing in my business.*

WHAT I WANT TO LEARN FROM MY CLIENTS:

- *To receive feedback on the current service levels my clients experience and understand what they feel is most valuable about their experience with us.*

- *To receive feedback on any areas that we may be able to improve on to become more referable.*

- *To gain our top client's insight into our future objectives and what advice they would have for where we will focus our efforts.*

- *To learn how our clients believe they can contribute to our growth plan and learn how they want to be involved in our growth.*

- *To get feedback on some of the changes that I plan to make in the coming year to the way that we provide service.*

Do you see how those goals and objectives from the earlier pages come back into play? That is why you cannot skip steps in the process. You will be putting those objectives in front of your clients. If you really think about this process, it makes sense for you and for your client. They will completely understand why it makes sense to involve your best clients in what you want to accomplish and with whom and to learn from them how best to achieve it. Your client will be very appreciative that you are involving them in the process. Now that you have explained why you decided to conduct the meetings and what you hope to accomplish by doing so, you need to let them know what will occur over the time that you have asked of them so that they know what to expect. The final portion of the Introduction may sound like this:

John, hopefully those objectives make sense to you. What I would like to do is spend the first few minutes here walking you through the first portion of my objectives. I want to share with you the business goals and objectives that we have for the future of the business. I want to talk to you about what services we want to focus on and what kind of clients we want to focus on. After walking you through that, I have about five questions I wanted to ask you to give me honest feedback on. Some of those questions are specifically about the business plan; others are more about our service in general. After our discussion, I have a brief questionnaire I wanted to ask you to complete so that I can get to the remainder of the issues that I want feedback on.

John, I want you to know how much I value your time. I know that asking this of you is a lot, and I do appreciate it. I want to use this whole process to continue to grow as a professional and provide the best experience possible for you. Does that all sound okay to you?

At this point, you will only be about five to seven minutes into the time you have asked of your client or referral relationship. They will have a very clear and sensible explanation of why you decided to ask for their time, what you want to accomplish with the process, and what will happen over the time that you have asked of them. The next step is to have a ten to fifteen minute "presentation" prepared of your business model, your business plan, and present it to insure that your clients know what you do, and who you want to grow your model with. First though, below is an example of the entire Introduction example put together:

John, I want to thank you for taking your time to come in and talk to me today. I want to begin by talking to you a little bit about what led me to conduct some of these meetings with my clients, what I hope to accomplish by doing so, and let you know exactly what to expect out of the time that I have asked of you.

As you know, I have been in business now for just over ten years. I have been very blessed to continue to build my business with many quality clients. When I look forward at the next ten years, I want to insure that I use what I have learned to continue to grow the business with the right kinds of clients. When I really think about the kinds of clients that we want to do business with, there are some characteristics that really jump out at me. I realize that we do business with a lot of different people, but, there are those select clients that just really seem to be a good fit for our business. Rather than continue on the path we have, I wanted to really focus on what our most respected clients value in our service, how we can improve the service, and on growing with the right kinds of clients.

I decided a good first step would be to clearly identify out of my 200 clients, which ones that I really enjoy serving and would really love to duplicate. This was a small portion of my client base. You are one of those clients. I wanted to get each of them to come in one-to-one and have a different kind of conversation than we usually do. I wanted to make sure that my top clients have a good feel for my vision for the company. I want to insure that my top clients understand what services we want to focus on and what kind of clients we want to grow the company with. Finally, and most importantly, I wanted to gain the insight my top clients can share on our value, areas we can improve, and their guidance on how to accomplish the growth. I wanted to walk you through the main objectives that I have for the meeting. I want to insure that you know what kind of feedback we are looking for and how I will use the feedback to become better at what I do.

As I mentioned, I realize that some of my top clients may not have a good feel for the vision of our company and where we want to take it in the future. This is obviously a big oversight on our part. We have a lot of talented clients and not having them involved in our business objectives is not a smart decision. I want to insure that through these meetings, our clients gain perspective about what we are trying to build and why. I also want to get feedback on certain issues. At this point, I want to walk you through the objectives that I outlined for these meetings. The primary goals and objectives for the meetings are:

WHAT I WANT TO SHARE WITH MY CLIENTS:

- *To clearly outline for my clients the focus of my business and what services that I really want to expand on.*

- *To clearly define for my clients the characteristics of our ideal client and why we want to focus our growth on that population.*

- *To discuss a few changes that I am considering implementing in my business.*

WHAT I WANT TO LEARN FROM MY CLIENTS:

- *To receive feedback on the current service levels my clients experience and understand what they feel is most valuable about their experience with us.*

- *To receive feedback on any areas that we may be able to improve on to become more referable.*

- *To gain our top client's insight into our future objectives and what advice they would have for where we will focus our efforts.*

- *To learn how our clients believe they can contribute to our growth plan and learn how they want to be involved in our growth.*

- *To get feedback on some of the changes that I plan to make in the coming year to the way that we provide service.*

Hopefully those objectives make sense to you John. What I would like to do is spend the first few minutes walking you through the first portion of my objectives. I want to share with you the business goals and objectives that we have for the future of the business. I want to talk to you about what services we want to focus on and what kind of clients we want

31

to target. After walking you through that, I have about five questions and I want to ask you to give me honest feedback. Some of those questions are specifically about the business plan; others are more about our service in general. After our discussion, I have a brief questionnaire I wanted to ask you to complete so that I can get feedback on remainder of the issues. John, I want you to know how much I value your time. I know that asking this of you is a lot, and I do appreciate it. I want to use this whole process to continue to grow as a professional and provide the best experience possible for you. Does that all sound okay to you?

Presentation

The second piece of your meeting should be a presentation of your business model and your business plan. It can be a one page outline. Most of the time, the organizations and professionals I work with assume that their clients understand what they do and for whom they do it. They are typically surprised to find out that clients often stereotype them into a much narrower service and expertise than they actually have. As I mentioned with the mortgage banker, his referral sources stereotyped him as an impaired credit risk expert, but he could do so much more.

I have met insurance agents who also provide investment guidance and their clients have no idea that these services are available. I have met real estate professionals who provide financing services and their clients don't know it. I have met accountants who provide business valuation and the business owner clients did not know it. Do your top clients really understand the depth of your service? Chances are that they don't really know how you position your business and your company. Chances are that they met you when they had a problem that you were there to solve. You probably solved their problem and they moved on thankful that you had. In the meantime, they are running in to all kinds of people that could use the services that they do not know that you have. This is the time to clarify what services you have.

If they are unclear about what it is that you do, I am certain that they are unsure about your clientele. If I came to my doctor because my foot hurt and he solved the problem, I would think he is a foot doctor. My friends and family could talk about their knee pain, their headaches and backaches, and I would not be able to recommend a good doctor. If their feet hurt, then I got the guy. Wouldn't my doctor benefit by insuring that I knew that he works on knees, backs, and heads? It really is that simple and it is simply that overlooked by most professions. We solve the problems that our clients come to us with and never sit them down to understand the challenges that we are capable of solving and who is ideal for our client base. While I will provide a complete example at the conclusion of this section, your presentation should include a few key pieces. Don't get hung up on the word "presentation." This does not need to be a power point presentation with audio and visual features. It can truly be an outline that you walk your clients through.

I would recommend that you walk your clients through a timeline of your business. I would walk them through how your business has evolved over the years and why you have made the changes that you have. Typically, the changes in your business involved trying to add value to people like them. I recommend that you cover where your business has been, where it currently is, and where you want to see it go in the future. Your clients' feedback is what is going to help you get there. They have to clearly understand your value proposition, what services you provide, and who most benefits from what you do. Below is an example of an insurance advisor who added investment services to their array of services. They feel like most of their clients look at them as just insurance experts when they could be working with their clients and others on their investment plans. Their focus is on the business owner marketplace. Here is the example of their presentation script:

John, as you know, we began in this industry focusing the majority of our attention on helping our clients manage their risk. We have always worked to be efficient for our clients at understanding the various insurance products and what needs they meet. While each of our clients has very specific needs, we have been able to work individually with them to insure that they had a plan to address those needs.

33

As we really began to look at the service that we provide to our client base, we realized that we were helping them protect the things that they had worked to acquire, but weren't involved with what they were working to build. We had a decision to make at that point. We decided that we would take the time and dedicate the resources to becoming investment advisors in addition to helping our clients with risk management. We knew how much both of these aspects of our clients' lives affect each other, but until we made that decision, we weren't really able to insure that both areas were working together for our clients.

When we added investment services to our business, we also knew that we would have a branding issue. We met many of our clients through the need they had to protect something with insurance and many of our key clients would not understand the investment aspect of our business. We knew that not only would that have an impact on our current clients maximizing their experience with us, but also on our ability to have our current clients identify friends and family that may need our help. If our clients only understood half of our service, they are not fully able to refer us.

We have continued to work on that aspect of our business but now find ourselves looking at how we want to grow the business moving forward. We have been blessed to continually grow and help people but we now must focus on a specific population to grow with to insure that our current clients don't experience poor services as a result of us helping anybody and everybody who comes through the door. We thought that it would be important for our clients to understand who we want to focus our business on moving forward, and why we feel that population can use our help.

We have added a specific kind of business insurance and investment service that is designed to meet several of the challenges that business owners face. Since you are a business owner, I thought that I would give you an overview of what the service is and how it works. Because we are looking to grow our business more specifically with the business owner population, your insight will be helpful. (Proceed with presentation of new business services)

This presentation has already covered several things. First and foremost, it establishes to the client base the fact that the advisor not only provides insurance services, but has an investment component to their business. As I said in previous sections, many of our clients may not know all of the services that we are capable of helping with. Explaining this timeline helps our clients understand how our business has evolved and is a natural opener to help that they may need; however, this part of the meeting is not about them, it is about us.

After talking about how the services evolved over the years, it is natural that your target client begins to evolve. It is natural to begin your business helping anyone who will talk to you. The problem is, many times we get trapped in this part of our business because we don't have a detailed plan to expand our business with a specific population. When you decide who you really want to serve, this is the natural next step to growing your business with that population. It is critical to let those who know you and trust you know that you have reached a specific point in your business where your products and services are focused on a specific population.

In the example above, the advisor went on to talk about the business insurance that they had added to the portfolio of services and how it can impact a business owner. During the discussion, which we will cover later, the client mentioned that they frequently network with a group of business owners that the advisor should talk to. They would probably find such services very valuable. The advisor followed up their clients request to talk to their network and gained two new clients immediately. This is the power of Feedback Marketing.

These meetings offer you the rare opportunity to clarify for your clients the services that you want to provide and who you want to provide them to. Most of the time, they are in contact regularly with such people but had previously not identified them as potential clients of yours. This is normally because they didn't fully understand the services that you provide. Remember—they don't spend their days wondering what is happening in your business. This advisor had acquired many clients through helping them with life insurance and that is the stereotype that the client will carry with them. Think of all of the missed opportunity we have by having our army of trusted relationships out marching blindly amongst all the opportunity for your business.

This presentation needs to be designed to remedy that issue. Clients should walk away from the meeting having a very clear idea of how your business has evolved over the years and with whom it has evolved. They must have a clear idea of who your company is focusing on serving and what resources you have to do so. Only then will they recognize their friends and family that have the challenges that your service is designed to solve.

The presentation can be in the form of a more formal power point but for me, it has always felt a little awkward with current clients. Just because you may not do a formal power point presentation does not mean you should sit down and wing it. Remember, you have the opportunity to have your clients full attention to clear up any misperception that may exist about the services that you provide and who you want to expand your company with, don't go in there without some clear points you want to cover.

As a review, you want to insure that you cover where your business has been, where your business currently is, and where you would like your business to go. Each of these phases should include a description of the services and the customer and how they have changed during the timeline. The most critical point is that your influential clients and referral relationships have a crystal clear picture of what services you want to provide and who you want to provide them to. This will have a dramatic impact on your referrals all without ever asking someone "who they know who can use your service."

At this point, you have explained to your clients why they are there and what you want to accomplish and you have given them an overview of where your business has been, where it is, and where you want it to go. Now is the most enjoyable part of the meeting, the discussion.

The Discussion

This is where you will change your business. Listening to your clients needs, their values, the resources they have to help you, and any of their valuable feedback will give you more follow up opportunity than you know what to do with. You can forget prospecting if you implement this process with 50 of your top relationships. You will have plenty of business right there in your office.

I was giving a speech yesterday to a Fortune 100 Company. Some of their top executives were in the room listening as I talked about the importance of listening. One of the executives at the end of speech said some variation of the following:

"I just want to chime in as a testimonial for what he is saying. The other day I had one of our top opportunities in the room. I asked them what was standing in the way of them achieving their objectives, and then I just listened. They told me everything I needed to know. Then I met with my staff and asked them what we could do to make their work environment more enjoyable — they gave me tons of ideas! This listening stuff works."

I know how silly and simple that sounds. The reality is from high level executives to the car salesman I met this morning, we have forgotten that it actually makes sense to ask questions and listen to the answers.

I called a car dealership this morning to ask if they had a very specific car. I had asked if they had Land Rover Range Rovers in white. This is the color that my wife wanted. The General Manager was on the phone. This guy operates the big Mercedes dealerships in town. His response to me was, "We don't, but I have the most beautiful white Lexus here that you will not believe. It is incredible. This car has been taken care of like nothing that I have ever seen. When would be a good time to get your little lady to come in and take a look at it?"

Notice, the only question he had asked was essentially, "When can you come in and look at the car that I have not even determined meets your needs, your price range, and anything you care about?"

What that guy should have said was, "I am sorry we don't have one in stock, can I ask you a question? What is important to you in the vehicle you are looking for?" It is that simple but that overlooked. I would have talked to him about what is important to us; our price range, why we are looking and I would bet he has tons of cars that would meet my needs. Instead, he tried to shove one down my throat. This is the perfect example of the way we are trained and the way we operate. Asking questions and listening will change your business.

In this particular meeting with a client, you will have about 20 to 25 minutes to ask questions and get feedback. You cannot go into the meeting assuming that you will figure out what questions you want to ask. You have got to prepare for this meeting to insure that you gain the feedback and accomplish the objectives that you have. I typically prepare about one question for every five minutes that we have to talk. Every question that you ask will lead to additional follow up questions on the same topic. If you want to have a discussion for 25 minutes, have five to six questions prepared to ask.

Your questions should fall around a few different categories to insure that you meet your objectives and get feedback on different areas of your business. Remember the objectives that you want to accomplish and these questions should come easily. There are a few common categories of questions.

Feedback on Value

The first area you should always focus on is the value that your clients receive from you. It is important for you to understand what they value most about the services that you provide to them. You should find value in understanding what was behind their decision to work with you and your firm. You should enjoy finding out what their experience has been like from the positive perspective. Not only will this be a positive way to kick off the discussion, but it will allow them to reinforce to themselves what they like about you and your company. It never hurts for a client to remind themselves of this. Some example questions may be:

When you think about the services that we provide for you and your business or family, what do you feel is the most valuable component of what we provide?

How has that value changed your business or your family's situation for the positive?

When you were considering who to help you with your challenges, what was your first impression of our firm and what made you decide on us to help?

These kinds of questions will reinforce to your clients the kinds of things they should tell other people about your service; however, may teach you a thing or two about your first impressions and the value you provide. I always have the first couple of questions prepared to discuss the value we provide. It is nice to hear about our value instead of constantly talking about it. Think about how simple that statement is. If you spent more than half of your time listening to what your value is and less than half of your time talking about it, would it impact your business?

Feedback on Areas to Improve Their Experience

These are the questions that many professionals fear. Many of us fear that if we ask our clients how we can improve, they may tell us! Any doctor will tell you that a symptom left untreated becomes an illness. Your clients service issues unnoticed will lead your clients to become one of your competitors clients.

As we talked about earlier, you should always be interested in how the boss thinks you can improve your performance. They are your boss and you truly should value any feedback that they can give. Any area that improves their experience will infinitely increase your ability to be referred. Inviting these clients to this meeting and taking the opportunity to ask these kinds of questions will immediately increase the image your clients have of you as a professional.

These questions need to be designed to find out what areas you may be able to improve so that your client enjoys a better experience. You will also want to ask if there are any areas of concern that may not have been addressed through the previous meetings you have had with a client. The financial advisor above found out from one of his clients that they had begun to explore using a product that provided more security with another firm. Until this meeting, they were unaware that he had expertise in those products and now that they did, he was able to schedule a meeting to discuss the issue. He made $44,000 providing a service that his client needed and was going to use someone else for. How frequently are your clients talking to your competitors because they don't know everything that you do?

If you get the feedback on these areas, you will improve if not perfect your retention while uncovering new opportunities with your existing client base. Examples of these kinds of questions include:

If we could work on one specific area that would make your experience with us better, what would that area be?

What areas of concern do you have that we may not have addressed in meetings? Do some areas leave you without complete peace of mind?

When you approach us for service or answers to your questions, how well do you feel that we resolve the issues in a way that you are comfortable with and completely feel served?

How do we make your experience one that you are compelled to tell other people about?

If you just look at the example questions in the previous section and these questions, ask yourself, "Would it be valuable for me to have the answers to these questions?" If you have read this far, I am sure that you have come to that conclusion; however, just think about how it will impact your business. Again, one hour per week with one client is all you need to do. You will have the answer to these questions from 50 of your best relationships with absolutely minimal effort. Think of the doors that will open up within your client base. The best part is that you haven't even started on the questions about how to grow your business. That is the third section that you need to focus on.

Feedback on Your Expansion Plans

In many industries we are trained to get referrals. Nearly everyone that I have met says that they have challenges in getting referrals. I am not different. We are all frustrated by that. This portion of your questioning is going to teach you how to approach your client base about referring the right kinds of clients for your business. I can tell you that the great part is that the hard part is already done. Chances are that they didn't even know who the right people are or that you had an expansion plan prior to this meeting. Now that they do, you need to ask for their advice on how to execute it.

If they are in the room with you, they are probably the kind of person that you would like to have more of. You can ask questions and they can give you feedback on behalf of people like them. Some examples of these questions include:

Knowing that we want to attract small business owners with our process, how would you approach business owners in our market?

Knowing that we want to leverage our relationships with our best clients, how would you recommend that we approach our clients about expanding our business with business owners?

How would you approach our clients in a way that is appropriate to meet other people who own businesses?

If you wanted to achieve the objectives that I laid out for you, what would you do today to start attracting more people like you?

These questions will accomplish a lot for you. You will learn what kind of access they have to potential clients. Many times they will recommend that you meet with them or come and give a speech to a group where they are a member. Other times they will give you more insight into how your target population views your service and what you should change about the way you approach a potential client.

In the example of our financial advisor, one of his Interactive Client Survey clients told him that they are the chair of a business owner association. This group of 100 meets monthly and is always looking for speakers with good information. "You ought to speak to our group about the investment market and what is happening today," he said.

Remember, this client didn't even understand that the advisor had expertise in investments or that he wanted to help business owners before he came to the meeting. Now he was offering him an audience with 100 individuals. All he had to do is follow up and get the date scheduled.

Good questions are designed to get the person answering the question to open up and talk about how they feel and how people like them feel. When a question is asked honestly and sincerely, it is answered the same way. If your clients can view you as a business and not just a person, they will give you the answers to any of the questions that you have. You don't need to worry about them being honest. If you are honest with them, they will reciprocate. If you go in to the meeting with a simple agenda to hit them up for referrals, you will come up empty. If you go in wanting to better understand how to approach your clients and your target market, you will be given more opportunity than you can handle. That is a great problem to have.

After having a great discussion, you will have a few additional questions that you want answered. Asking your clients to fill out a brief written questionnaire will give you the remainder of the feedback that you want in a format that you can review when you have set aside the time. The problem many of my consulting clients run into is that the discussion is so enjoyable, they run with that and then have to try to squeeze in the questionnaire. This should not happen. The questionnaire will tell you even more about what you need to know to grow your business. You need to treat it with the importance that it deserves.

The Questionnaire

As you will see in the following sections on how to manage focus groups, questionnaires are golden. When you write a good questionnaire, you will get all of the information that you need to improve and expand your business. You will also get information from the person who completed it that will allow you to follow up with them and offer them something that they find truly valuable. This will work with both clients and prospective clients as you will see. For our purposes in this section, I will continue to speak about the questionnaire as it relates to the Interactive Client Surveys.

When you review the objectives that you set out to accomplish at the beginning of this process, you will see that you have already created the foundation for your discussion and questionnaire questions. I recommend that you review each objective and write a few questions that you would love to ask your clients specific to that objective. Initially, don't worry about how you word the questions. These initial questions may be as rough as:

Do my clients understand what I do?

Why don't my clients refer me more business?

Why aren't some of my best clients happy?

Writing down questions like these will develop an overall theme for the line of questions. After writing the complete list of questions that will help you identify what questions you really want to focus on, you will need to decide which questions are appropriate for the discussion portion of your meeting and which questions are better suited for the questionnaire. A general guide is that questions involving specific issues should generally be on the questionnaire whereas the 30,000 foot questions like the ones in the previous section would be more appropriate for discussion. Questionnaires should be a combination of two types of questions; open ended and rating scale questions. Open ended questions are those that cannot be answered by a one word response. These are questions like: Do you feel that we provide a valuable service? This question will not get you the information that you seek. This question is better asked: What do you see as the primary value that our service offers to you and your family and why? Asked that way, the respondent has no option but to give a multi-sentence answer on a questionnaire. Questions that require a lengthy sentence response are open ended questions.

The second type of question that will be effective on the questionnaire are rating scale questions. Rating scale questions traditionally measure how someone feels about something and how strongly they feel about it. You want to be careful with these kinds of questions as they don't cover why the respondent feels the way that they do. Open ended questions are good for answering that. An example of a rating scale question would be:

On a scale of 1 to 10, how quickly do you feel that we respond to the needs that you have when you contact us?

1 2 3 4 5 6 7 8 9 10
Not at All Quickly   Somewhat Quickly   Very Quickly

Rating scale questions are much less personal and often resemble what you would see on a survey. For your purposes of accomplishing the objectives that you have, you will want a good mix of rating scale and open ended questions for your clients to complete. Remember your objectives when authoring your questionnaire. Again, with the example above of the insurance agent turned investment advisor, there were very specific goals for the meeting. The first was that the advisor wanted to insure that the client had a good idea of what services his company offered, who he wanted to offer them to, and then get feedback on his service and how to accomplish his goals. His questionnaire follows:

QUESTIONNAIRE SAMPLE

Name _____

We want to thank you for your participation in our Interactive Client Surveys. You have been asked to participate because we value and respect your input and feedback. This questionnaire is designed to gain additional feedback on questions that are vital to our growth and providing the level of service we desire to provide to our clients. We sincerely appreciate your thorough and honest answers to these questions. The answers will be used to help us provide an exceptional experience to our valued clients.

1. How would you recommend that we approach the topic of growing our practice and getting referrals from our top clients in a comfortable way?

2. What is the one positive thing that has changed in the last couple of years that has had a significant impact on the way you feel about your financial future?

3. In meeting our clients and new clients, how do you feel our attire should change if at all to insure we portray a professional image:

1 2 3 4 5 6 7 8 9 10
Less Formal   Current Attire   More Formal
(golf slacks/shirt)   (slacks/dress shirt)   (jacket/tie)

4. On a scale of 1-10, how accessible do you feel we are to answer the questions that you have?

1 2 3 4 5 6 7 8 9 10
Not very accessible   Somewhat accessible   Very accessible

5. When you contact our firm, how well do you feel we resolve any issues that you may face?

1 2 3 4 5 6 7 8 9 10
Not well   Somewhat well   Extremely well

6. What is the one improvement that our firm could make to improve the experience that you have with us?

7. What is your most pressing concern with achieving the financial objectives that you and your family have?

Understanding how to improve the way that you communicate will. Insure that you are getting to both the former and latter.

This questionnaire should be completed as part of the meeting that you have with your client. You should give them approximately ten minutes alone to complete it. Your client will be absolutely fine taking the time to complete it thoroughly at your office. If they leave with the questionnaire, you will not see it again. They love you while they are there, they forget about you when they leave. Insure that you block the time to get this completed.

Conclusion on Structuring the Meeting

A meeting without structure is not a meeting at all. You can go from corporation to corporation all throughout the country and see thousands of highly paid executives sitting in meetings that have no clear objectives, no clear goals, and accomplish nearly nothing. Don't let your one time meeting with a client this year become one of those meetings.

Applying solid structure to how you will introduce the meeting and the objectives for it, the presentation that you will give, the discussion questions you want to ask, and what questions you want a written response to will reap rewards beyond any of your marketing. When you structure your meeting well, your client will leave feeling appreciated and as though they contributed something to the clear objectives and purpose that you had for the meeting. Once you have developed your clear cut objectives and the method for reaching them, you are prepared to begin scheduling meetings.

Step 5 - Scheduling the Meeting

At this point, you have clearly outlined the challenges you face, your goals and objectives, and who can help you with the goals and objectives. A typical meeting schedule has been provided. Now comes the easy part, scheduling the time.

While most of the organizations and professionals that I consult with would say that many of their clients would come in with a simple phone call and a request for some time — that is not what you want to do. You have to remember that this kind of a meeting should look and feel different. You don't want a client who gladly shows up for an hour of your time and then has no real understanding of why they are attending the meeting. At best, you will spend several minutes talking about nothing because the client thinks they are there to chat.

It is important to carefully craft the language that you will use either in person or via the phone to schedule the time with your client. This is a highly structured meeting and has a highly structured purpose. It should feel that way when you call to invite them. Invitations for this kind of a meeting have two components. The first component is a simple request to explain to your client why you want them to come in. The second is an explanation of why you are conducting Interactive Client Surveys.

Permission to Explain

When someone answers the phone, they are not prepared to listen. The first objective in the invitation script is to greet your client, identify yourself, tell them briefly why you are calling, and get permission to explain further. An example is:

> *Hey John, this is Dan Allison. How are you? Great, hey I was calling you because I am conducting a few special meetings with a select portion of my client base. Do you have a minute for me to explain what I am doing and what I want to accomplish to see if you would participate?*

This simple opening will take your client from an inactive bystander in the phone call to an active listener who is ready to hear what you are doing and why. Calling them a "select client" is also important because they know this call isn't going out to everyone.

Explaining Your Purpose

The second piece of the invitation should be a brief discussion of why you want to conduct some Interactive Client Surveys and what you hope to accomplish. You should also briefly cover what will happen during the time that you asked for. An example would be:

> *Thanks John, as we sit down and look at the company's objectives moving forward, we have decided to involve our top clients a little bit more in our goals and objectives. We decided that it would really help us to get some feedback from some of our most respected relationships. We primarily are trying to get an idea of what is important to our clients; how we can improve their experience, and get some advice on our future plans. You are someone that I have a great deal of respect for and would appreciate your participation in one of the meetings. I am simply asking a few clients to come in for an hour where I will discuss further our plans and ask some questions to get the honest feedback and guidance that I am looking for. John, I know you are busy and I respect your time. Would you considering helping us in this effort?*

If your clients say no to this, there are much bigger issues that need to be identified as soon as possible. Combining these two sections together will leave you with a script like the one below. This script will encompass most of you who are implementing this process:

> *Hey John, this is Dan Allison. How are you? Great, hey I was calling you because I am conducting a few special meetings with a select portion of my client base. Do you have a minute for me to explain what I am doing and what I want to accomplish to see if you would participate?*

> *Thanks John, as we sit down and look at the company's objectives moving forward, we have decided to involve our*

48

top clients a little bit more in our goals and objectives. We decided that it would really help us to get some feedback from some of our most respected relationships. We primarily are trying to get an idea of what is important to our clients; how we can improve their experience, and get some advice on our future plans. You are someone that I have a great deal of respect for and would appreciate your participation in one of the meetings. I am simply asking a few clients to come in for an hour where I will discuss further our plans and ask some questions to get the honest feedback and guidance that I am looking for. John, I know you are busy and I respect your time. Would you considering helping us in this effort?

I recommend that most of my clients make the phone calls once a month and schedule one Interactive Client Survey per week. This assumes of course that you have 40-50 quality relationships with clients or professionals who can refer you clients. Both are good populations to meet with. If you simply implemented that recommendation, you would spend less than a half hour on the phone per month scheduling the appointments, and four hours per month implementing the appointments. Do you think by the end of the year that those 50 meetings and surveys will teach you a great deal and lead to more opportunity? Of course they will. You will learn an incredible amount while gaining more business.

The number one area that I see professionals fall short is in not blocking the time to schedule the appointments. You can come up with all sorts of reasons why you can't make calls. Don't fall into that trap. Block your call day every single month and schedule an appointment every single week. Most of the things that are keeping you busy don't increase your clients' value or gain you more business. These meetings need to be a priority.

After scheduling the appointments, you will need to insure that the setting is right for the kind of outcome that you want to achieve. You will want to set the appropriate stage for the meeting. The next step to implementing successful Interactive Client Surveys is to conduct the meeting with the appropriate setting and resources.

Step 6 - Setting the Stage

For many of you, this will be the first time that you have asked your key relationships to come in specifically to talk about you and your business. We are used to talking about the client or how we can help others. Don't over think what you have asked your client to do. Chances are, they value what you provide to them and they are eager to help you in any way that they can. You probably have just never given them the way to do so.

The first key to having a successful meeting is to insure that you are prepared prior to the meeting with the client or referral relationship. Many of my clients have told me that they felt rushed and when I looked at their schedules, they scheduled meetings right up until the minute their client was coming in for this meeting. Give yourself some buffer time to insure that you have set things up well. There are a few important pieces to insure are in place prior to the meeting.

The Environment

The most important aspect of your Interactive Client Survey is that you conduct them in an environment that is professional, free of distractions, and most importantly, private. This is ideal in your office or a conference room. My preference is a conference room because our offices are often full of clutter that serves as a reminder of all the things that we have to do.

This meeting should feel as though it was well planned (because it should be) and that it is very important to you (because it is). An advisor who worked closely with me called me in to role play his first Interactive Client Survey. When I arrived at his offices, he informed me that the conference room was being used so we would use his office (poor planning). In his office, he had memorabilia from every sporting event he had attended in his life hanging from the walls and stacked up on shelves. Paper was thrown all over his desk. The office was a wreck. I felt like I was interrupting something. This is not the environment at all that I am talking about.

After we sat down he asked if he could get me something to drink. I said coffee and we waited for five minutes while someone got me coffee. Five minutes that could have been spent giving him feedback. As we began our discussion he had papers in front of him but no papers in front of me which left me wondering what he was reading. The phone continued to ring and to top it off, his cell phone vibrated (which was sitting on the table) and he looked at it to see who it was!

While you may be thinking, that sounds disastrous, look around your office and think about the meetings you conduct with your clients on a regular basis. How many of those things are happening in your office. This was all a sign of bad planning. Your environment should be clean and absolutely free of distraction. If you don't have a conference room available, insure the distractions in your office are shut off. Cell phones don't need to be on "vibrate," they need to be on "off." Unless your wife is going into labor at any second, there is very little that cannot wait an hour. Turn off your computer so your screen saver doesn't have fish floating up and down on it. Insure your office phone does not ring and cannot ring because you have either put it on Do Not Disturb or unplugged it. Finally, insure that your office staff know that you are not to be bothered under any circumstance.

We live in a world of constant interruption. We have allowed it to become so normal in our lives that we don't notice when it happens and we don't understand how insulting it is to the "important" person that we are with. Never give your client or referral relationship the opinion that something is more important than them and their time. I would recommend that you even ask if they mind shutting off their cell phone if possible. That will depend on your relationship with your client but it is great when you have an hour of absolutely uninterrupted time.

The Paper

Before the meeting, you should prepare a folder with the information that will be important. There are a few pieces that need to be in there and some that are optional based on what you are presenting. Having this folder prepared for your client not only shows great planning, but it will keep you on task.

Agenda

First, you will want to have an agenda for the meeting. Agendas tell your clients that you have very specific things that you want to accomplish and will insure that you keep on track. If you ever want to insure that you are in control of a meeting, bring an agenda and those you are meeting with will likely assume that you are running the meeting. The agenda should cover the four aspects of the meeting that you requested. First, you should have five minutes for establishing your purpose and your objectives. I recommend that you actually list your objectives for the client so that you can walk them through the objectives during your introduction. Next, you will move on to an overview of the content that you want to discuss or the presentation information. After that, you have some discussion questions that you want to ask. Finally, you will have a written questionnaire that you want them to complete.

On the next page I have written a sample of an Interactive Client Survey agenda:

AGENDA FOR INTERACTIVE CLIENT SURVEY
DATE

5:30P-5:35 p.m.   INTRODUCTION AND OVERVIEW

      -What lead us to conduct these meetings?
      -What will happen over the course of the hour?
      -Covering our key objectives:

WHAT I WANT TO SHARE WITH MY CLIENTS:

- *To clearly outline for my clients the focus of my business and what services that I really want to expand on.*

- *To clearly define for my clients the characteristics of our ideal client and why we want to focus our growth on that population.*

- *To discuss a few changes that I am considering implementing in my business.*

WHAT I WANT TO LEARN FROM MY CLIENTS:

- *To receive feedback on the current service levels my clients experience and understand what they feel is most valuable about their experience with us.*

- *To receive feedback on any areas that we may be able to improve on to become more referable.*

- *To gain our top clients' insight into our future objectives and what advice they would have for focusing on our efforts.*

- *To learn how our clients believe they can contribute to our growth plan and learn how they want to be involved in our growth.*

- *To get feedback on some of the changes that I plan to make in the coming year to the way that we provide service.*

5:35-5:55 p.m.   OVERVIEW OF BUSINESS AND CHALLENGES

5:55-6:20 p.m.   DISCUSSION OF FEEDBACK QUESTIONS

6:20-6:30 p.m.   COMPLETE QUESTIONNAIRE

6:30 p.m.   ADJOURN

Thank you for your participation

Presentation

The second thing that you should include in the folder that you give the client is something relevant to the content or presentation. As we discussed in the presentation section, this can be a formal presentation piece that you are looking for feedback on or simply an overview of your business with some bullet points.

Again, this is not only to show the client that you have thought through this process, but it will keep you on track and insure that you stick to the agenda.

Questionnaire

Put a copy of the questionnaire inside of the folder behind the agenda. You don't want the questionnaire to be the first thing that they see because they will be distracted by the questions and may be overwhelmed by the idea of having to do work in the meeting. Insure that the questionnaire is all the way to the back of the folder behind any other presentation pieces and agendas you may have.

With these things in place, you should be prepared for your client to arrive. I always have my assistant place a confirmation call to insure that I do not get the environment set up and all of the information together for a no-show. It is acceptable to make your own confirmation calls if you don't have an assistant. Once your room is free of distractions and your information is ready, it is time to conduct the meeting.

Step 7 - Conducting the Meeting

We have spent a great deal of time talking in detail about preparing the meeting. If that is all done, the meeting will be the fun part. The number one mistake that I see advisors make in these meetings is that they don't give them the attention that they deserve. Whether it is because they don't do them consistently, or they really don't take setting the appropriate stage seriously. Professionals should treat these meetings as though they are the only marketing opportunity that is used. The reality is, when you do them well they are the only marketing activity you will need to do.

With the office clean, a folder professionally organized and minutes to spare, your client will arrive for the meeting. When your client arrives, don't have an assistant show them back to your office. I am always slightly offended when the person that I am meeting with doesn't find me worthy of personally coming out to greet me. We are taught frequently to position ourselves as the ultimate professional. This is not one of those times. Come and greet the client. Deliver any refreshments before the meeting starts so that you do not have any distractions during your meeting.

Ask the client to have a seat and open the folder that they have placed in front of them. It is important not to get engaged in a lot of small talk. If they are higher level people and literally have only blocked an hour, you cannot afford to waste 15 minutes talking about golf. Get right into the agenda. Begin with your Introduction:

John, I want to thank you for taking your time to come in and talk to me today. I want to begin by talking to you a little bit about what led me to conduct some of these meetings with my clients, what I hope to accomplish by doing so, and let you know exactly what to expect out of the time that I have asked of you.

As you know, I have been in business now for just over ten years. I have been very blessed to continue to build my business with many quality clients. When I look forward to the next ten years, I want to insure that I use what I have learned to continue to grow the business with the right kinds of clients. When I think about the kinds of clients that we want to provide services to, there are some characteristics that really jump out at me. I realize that we do business with a lot of different people, but, there are those select clients who just really seem to be a good fit for our business. Rather than continue on the path we have, I wanted to focus on what our most respected clients' value in our service, how we can improve the service, and thus grow with the right type of clients.

I decided a good first step would be to clearly identify out of my 200 clients, which ones I really enjoy serving and which ones I would really love to duplicate. This was a small portion of my client base. You are one of those clients. I wanted to ask each of them to come in one-to-one and have a different kind of conversation than we usually do. I wanted to make sure that my top clients have a good feel for my vision for the company. I want to insure that my top clients understand what services we want to focus on and the kind of clients we hope to attract. Finally, and most importantly, I wanted to gain my top clients' insight on our value, in areas we can improve, and their guidance on how to foster growth and continuous improvement.

I want to walk you through the main objectives that I have for the meeting. I want to insure that you know what kind of feedback we are looking for and how I will use the feedback to become better at what I do.

As I mentioned, I realize that some of my top clients may not have a good feel for the vision of our company and what our future looks like. This is obviously a big oversight on our part. We have many talented clients and not having them involved in our business objectives is not a smart decision. I want to insure that through these meetings, our clients gain perspective about what we are trying to build and why. I also want to get feedback on certain issues. At this point, I want to walk you through the objectives that I outlined for these meetings. The primary goals and objectives for the meeting are:

WHAT I WANT TO SHARE WITH MY CLIENTS:

- *To clearly outline the focus of my business and what services that I want to expand.*

- *To clearly define the characteristics of our ideal client and why we want to focus our growth on that population.*

- *To discuss a few changes that I am considering implementing in my business.*

WHAT I WANT TO LEARN FROM MY CLIENTS:

- *To receive feedback on the current service levels my clients experience and understand what they feel is most valuable about their experience with us.*

- *To receive feedback on any areas that we may be able to improve on to become more referable.*

- *To gain our top client's insight into our future objectives and what advice they would have for where we will focus our efforts.*

- *To learn how our clients believe they can contribute to our growth plan and learn how they want to be involved in our growth.*

- *To get feedback on some of the changes that I plan to make in the coming to the services that we provide.*

John, hopefully those objectives make sense to you. What I would like to do is spend the first few minutes here walking you through the first portion of my objectives. I want to share with you the future business goals and objectives we have. I want to talk to you about what kind of clients we want to target. After walking you through that, I have about five questions. And I would like your honest feedback. Some of those questions are specifically about the business plan; others are more about our service in general. After our discussion, I have a brief questionnaire. John, I want you to know how much I value your time. I know that asking this of you is a lot, and I appreciate it. I want to use this process to continue to grow as a professional and provide the best experience possible for you. Does that all sound okay to you?

At this point, your client or referral relationships will have an excellent understanding of why you have chosen to call them in today. They will not feel like they are there to be hounded about referrals, but more as a sounding board for a professional that they respect. They will feel flattered that they were one of the people that you thought enough of to ask to participate in the meeting and are all ears for the overview of your company or your presentation:

John, as you know, we began in this industry focusing the majority of our attention on helping our clients manage their risk. We have always worked to be efficient at understanding the various insurance products and what needs they meet. While each of our clients has very specific needs, we have been able to work individually with them to insure that they had a plan to address those needs.

As we really began to look at the service that we provide to our client base, we realized that we were helping them protect the things that they had worked to acquire, but weren't involved with what they were working to build. We had a decision to make at that point. We decided that we would take the time and dedicate the resources to becoming investment advisors in addition to helping our clients with risk management. We knew how much both of these aspects of our clients' lives affect each other, but until we made that decision, we weren't really able to insure that both areas were working together for our clients.

When we added investment services, we also knew that we would have a branding issue. We met many of our clients because of the need they had to protect something with insurance. Many of our key clients would not understand the investment aspect of our business. We knew that not only would that have an impact on our current clients maximizing their experience with us, but also on our ability to have our current clients identify friends and family that may need our help. If our clients only understood half of our service, they are not fully able to refer us.

We have continued to work on that aspect of our business but now find ourselves looking at how we want to continue to grow the business. We have been blessed to continually grow and help people but we now must focus on a specific target population. This will insure that our current clients don't experience poor services as a result of us helping anybody and everybody who comes through the door. We thought that it would be important for our clients to understand who we want to target and why we feel that population can use our help.

While this is an abbreviated example, I am sure that you get the idea. The first half of this meeting is about you taking control to explain your objectives, and presenting anything that you want to insure that your clients and referral relationships understand your business, your services, and your future objectives. After giving them an overview of the content, you will move into your discussion. The discussion is really the critical point in the meeting. The discussion is where your client will either feel like they had an impact on what you wanted to accomplish, or that you actually just called them in so that you could present something to them.

You should have a list of four to five questions you would like to ask the client to discuss. Remember, if they can tell that you genuinely want the answers to the questions that you are asking, they will be happy to engage in the discussion. The most common errors professionals make is that they don't listen and they hate silence. When you ask your client a question, give some time for them to answer. Remember, this is the first time that the question has ever been asked of them. You want them to think about the answer that they give. You will need to transition from your presentation or content to the discussion with a couple of simple sentences. I recommend that you say:

John, that is essentially the content that I wanted to share with you today. Did that make sense to you? Good, I have prepared about five questions that I wanted to ask the clients that I selected to be part of this survey process. I asked you to participate in these meetings because I felt like you would be honest with me. John, what do you feel is the most valuable service that we provide to your family and why do you feel that way?

You have asked your first question of your client. Now, you just need to sit back, jot down some notes, and listen to your clients talk. Again, there may be some silence as they think about the answers to the questions that you ask during the discussion. Don't worry about silence. There is absolutely nothing uncomfortable about waiting for your clients to answer. You will see that once the opinions start flowing, you will have additional questions. It is fine to ask follow up questions as they give you their answers. Your goal should be to truly understand how the client feels about the question and why. When people are interviewed, they feel important. Don't worry about your client, they are feeling fine about being asked questions.

It is easy to have the client answer the first question and then get off track by asking follow up questions that take you a completely different direction from your plan. While it is okay to explore a little, keep the discussion questions that you wanted to discuss in front of you to insure that you get to each of them. You don't want to learn what they value, what you can improve, and what they think of the experience that they have without ever getting to the feedback on how to approach clients about expansion or referrals.

As you begin having this discussion with your client, it is likely that you will run out of time. I constantly have clients tell me that they were enjoying the meeting and the discussion too much that they ran over on time. While the verbal feedback is important, the written feedback is gold. If you run over during the discussion, chances are they will feel rushed in completing the written questionnaire and you will get brief answers. Insure that you stop the discussion with 10 minutes remaining to complete the questionnaire. You can transition to the questionnaire by saying something like:

John, your feedback has been very helpful and I wish I had asked you for more time so that we could continue the discussion. I want to insure out of respect for your time that I allow you the time necessary to fill out the written questionnaire. While I am learning a lot from my discussions with select clients, these questionnaires have been incredibly helpful for us. I am going to go ahead and grab something out in the lobby. I will leave you in here for about 10 minutes to complete the written questionnaire. John, I can't tell you how much your guidance means to me. Please be as thorough as you can.

At that point, leave the room. You would be a distraction if you stayed in the office. They will not mind completing a questionnaire at all. At this point, they feel as though they have been helpful and they will give a lot of attention to the questionnaire. Remember, mailed surveys are for car dealers and restaurants; this is a lot more important.

Return to the room about ten minutes later and collect their questionnaire. Let them know how helpful their time has been and how excited you are to take their feedback as well as the rest of your clients, and implement change in your business. If they have offered up resources or referrals as we had discussed, let them know that you will follow up with them. Nearly every meeting will end with some form of action to be taken. Many times you will need to follow up on opportunities that your client offered during the discussion. Other times, you will have uncovered a need that they have that you need to follow up on. Leave your client with a hand shake and a sincere thank you. Let them know when and how you will follow up on the discussion.

Some professionals give their clients a small token of their appreciation. I completely recommend that you do. And, I do not suggest a gift card to a barbeque joint. Give them something that really shows that you know what they value and what they enjoy. I know a lot of great business leaders who take pride in being excellent parents. Get them a $20 picture frame for their office to hold pictures of their kids. Another idea is a business book of inspirational quotes. Give them something that is valuable well beyond what it costs you. I always write a personal hand-written note in a book or on a gift thanking them again.

When your clients walk out of these meetings, they should feel better about themselves than when they came in. They should be flattered because they were selected; they should feel important because they gave great advice; they should have loved the little meaningful gift that you gave. They will walk out feeling as though you gave them something when the reality is the other way around. You will learn a great deal from every one of these meetings.

As I mentioned earlier, these meetings should occur weekly. You should involve each client that you respect once a year if possible. They will always enjoy the conversation and you can always update them on the things that are going on in your business. The key to insuring that these meetings are not just fun, but incredibly effective is how you use the information you gather and how you follow up with your clients after they have given you their time and their feedback.

Step 8 - The Follow Up

One of the great things about conducting Interactive Client Surveys consistently is that the follow up to the meetings is effective and extremely manageable. Unlike many group activities you are able to simply block about a half hour to take the action steps necessary to insure that your client knows that their time was spent for a purpose, that it was appreciated, and to take the next steps toward following up on opportunity that they offered.

I always recommend that you should block the half hour just after the discussion to organize notes, your thoughts, and review the questionnaire that the client left behind. I always try to analyze three specific areas between the discussion and the questionnaire:

- Did I learn more about how my client perceives my value?
- Did I learn how to improve the experience that my client has so that I can increase my ability to be referred?
- Did I identify any resources that they have available to them to introduce me to the right kind of people?

Did you notice in the examples provided in this section that I focused equally on these three points? I want to insure that I have a clear understanding of how they view my value, how to improve their experience, and how to approach them about expanding my business. These three categories are the main measuring stick that I recommend. If you say "no" to any of the three, you need to revisit the discussion questions and questionnaire questions to insure that you are asking questions that cover that area. You have got to have a balance of all three.

During the half hour after the interview, I will break my notes into these three categories so that I can begin to design my follow up. At the end of a meeting, my notes may say something like:

WHAT IS MY VALUE

The Client:

- Believes that I worked to develop trust and have always been straightforward with them.
- Feels that I was a good listener and carefully consider alternatives before giving my advice.
- Sees my service as unique and very valuable to the needs of business owners.
- Did not understand that I provide investment and insurance services.

WHAT CAN I IMPROVE

The Client:

- Believes that more one-to-one time may help alleviate some of their concerns.
- Thought that I sometimes confuse them with information and over assume their level of understanding.
- Stated that they have been considering some alternative products to what they have, and wanted to set a time to discuss those additional products.

WHAT OPPORTUNITY MAY EXIST

The Client:

- Said that I need to be more consistent in communicating the business part of my practice and defining who I want to meet.
- Had a friend who owns a business that was looking for good resources to help them.
- Is a chair of business owner association and recommended that I speak at an upcoming event.

These are the kind of comments that will be extremely common. I will use each in my approach to the client. First, I want to insure that I thank them for finding value in the services that I provide. Second, I want to insure that the advice to improve did not fall through the cracks. I will follow up on their needs, especially the fact that they want to learn about new products. Finally, I want to follow up on the friend that may need help and the speaking opportunity with my client. After writing these notes down, I wrap my half hour by identifying clear action steps and scheduling the time to complete the tasks. It should not take more than an additional half hour but is certainly worth it. I would much rather follow up with a current client on a friend that needs help and a speaking engagement than spend a half hour cold calling.

There are several methods of follow up after the Interactive Client Survey. The key is not in how you follow up. Rather, it is that you do follow up and that there is a clear action that takes place. The main methods of follow up are by phone or in a letter. My preference is to do both. A letter shows that I took the time to sit down and write a very specific thank you letter to them, and a phone call allows me to schedule the next action.

An example of the letter I would send based on the notes above is on the following page.

Dear John,

I want to thank you for participating in my Interactive Client Survey. I had asked you for the time because I have a high level of respect for you and knew that you would bring good advice with you. I want to let you know that you really delivered for me.

First, I want to let you know that I am glad to hear that your family feels that I am trustworthy and a good listener. These are skills that I have worked hard at and I am glad to see that it doesn't go unnoticed. I am also glad to hear that you feel my focus on business owners is the right move. Your feedback in that regard was really helpful.

I want to let you know that I will be calling you to schedule a time with you and Lisa to discuss the issues you brought up regarding meeting and discussing specific products. I agree that the market has changed and we should definitely be doing that for you.

Finally, thank you for your kind offer to recommend your friend who owns a business to me. As you know, I will certainly lend them an ear and give them any advice that I can. I will follow up with you on the same phone call to schedule an appointment regarding your friend, and speaking to the Business Owner Association. Your ideas and your resources are so helpful. The fact that you shared them with me is very much appreciated. I will look forward to calling you and meeting with you and Lisa again.

Respectfully,

Dan Allison

Obviously I will follow up that letter with the phone call I mentioned and follow through with my promise. If you think about this one example, I accomplished a lot with a simple meeting:

- I increased the satisfaction of a respected client by simply involving them.
- I sealed the retention of that client.
- I clarified my value statement and identified my prospects for my client.
- I created a client who has a clear vision of individuals to recommend to me.
- I learned what my client finds valuable about my service.
- I identified areas of concern that can easily be addressed.
- I identified a need that may lead to additional service and revenue.
- I received an opportunity to meet a new client.
- I received an invitation to speak to 100 potential new clients.

These are not abnormal results. There is so much opportunity in your business model. There are so many connections and resources within your client base. Think of all of the executives, marketing experts, social networkers, business owners and managers that exist in your client base. The power of their knowledge and advice is limitless.

In Conclusion

I often begin keynote speeches or workshops by asking the audience one question; "If you were able to hire the 50 most sought after experts on how to duplicate your most valuable clients for free, would you?" Every time I ask it is a resounding "Yes!" That is what this process will allow you to do. I am a consultant to lots of companies. I work with publicly traded companies, and I work with individual professionals. An hour with me is nothing compared to an hour with your best client.

The 50 best referral coaches may be good at giving you scripting and different ideas on how to work with clients but the real answers lie within your clients. Each of them is unique. No one approach works for each client. You need to engage them in your business and involve them in your decision making. Give them the respect that they deserve when it comes to asking for feedback. Never send a self addressed stamped envelope to someone that is influential and you would love to clone.

If you simply take the one example in the last section and multiply it by 50, you will never market your services again in the traditional sense. The time that you spend at trainings about prospecting new clients or reading clever techniques to gain new business will be replaced with meaningful client discussions and doors being consistently opened by them.

If you simply used this one technique with your current clients, you would transform your business; however, I know that not every business is alike. Therefore I have included two more strategies in this book. Both of the strategies in the following pages mirror the philosophies and the simplicity of this approach. They are both equally cost effective and more importantly, professional and fun. Interactive Client Surveys will catapult your business. Interactive Client Surveys coupled with focus groups can provide you the information you need to transform your business.

FM

CLIENT CENTERED FOCUS GROUPS

Let Your Clients Tell You How to Duplicate Them and Keep Them Happy

YOU WILL GAIN

- Valuable feedback on the experience your clients have
- Valuable feedback on how to improve your services
- A client with a clear idea of your business objectives and your ideal prospects
- A client who understands their role in helping you achieve those objectives
- Improved retention through listening to the clients real needs
- More referrals from being top of mind with the client
- A stronger relationship with existing valuable clients
- An unprecedented way to introduce existing clients to new products and services

CLIENT CENTERED FOCUS GROUPS

One of my favorite shows that was cancelled prematurely was called The American Inventor. It was simple in premise. People from all over the world who considered themselves "inventors" would come in front of a panel of judges to show the judges the wonderful widget that they created. They would come out with flashy presentations and demonstrate the problems that the widget was designed to solve and in most cases demonstrate a working prototype.

On the show, the judges would commonly ask the contestants how much of their own money they had invested in their efforts. The typical answer was north of $100,000 and was normally followed by the story of losing their home and living in their car because they knew that they had the next great invention.

As with most of those shows, they denied most of the people but chose a small group of maybe 20 whose inventions showed potential. The first step in assessing what potential the product had was to conduct focus groups. These people had invested hundreds of thousands of dollars in their inventions. Certainly they had completed focus groups to see what their potential buyer would think, right? Of course not. That makes too much sense. My favorite part of the show was watching the inventor as focus groups identified the strengths and weaknesses of the invention. The weaknesses were so obvious to the focus groups but so profound to the inventor. How could the inventor not have asked their target consumer what was valuable to them before living in their car? They could have saved their home.

Focus groups are such a simple concept. You get a small group of like-minded people in a room. These people commit their time to come in and hear a presentation or see a product demonstration or simply just to discuss a topic. The company conducting the group uses the information to be valuable to its target consumers. This concept is profoundly simple. Identify the kinds of people that you really want to do more business with, take the time to listen to what they value about what you have, what they don't like or what you are missing, and then take the necessary steps to become more valuable. It seems like something that every business owner should have to do. Nearly all of the Fortune 500 Companies engage overpaid firms to come in and conduct focus groups. If you don't make that list, chances are that you are not doing them.

The topic of focus groups is not taught in school. Yet, they can have such a dramatic impact on the way that we do business and how we serve the people that our livelihood depends on. Why don't we spend more time understanding the people that we serve?

I did a consulting project with a large bank. They had a lot of wealthy customers and a great brand in their market place. They had added investment and insurance services to their brand and for three years had struggled to get any of their clients to engage in the service. Imagine the frustration of the investment division as they watched bags of money walk in all day long, but never stop to talk to them. They decided that it was time to conduct focus groups to introduce their banking clients to the service and learn how to best approach the client base about what was available to them.

We simply called some long-standing relationships and told them we were conducting a few small groups of trusted and valued clients to get some of their feedback on a service that the bank was working to promote. The banking clients were happy to oblige. We sat in the focus group with ten solid clients. I explained that the bank had added this service as a value to the client base but very few seemed to be seeing value in the service. Our quest was simple. We needed to find out how to approach the banking clients about the services and what they would value from the investment division. We talked briefly about what services the investment division offered and how they were unique and then began the discussion.

Imagine the surprise when the group all agreed that the primary reason people were not using the division was that none of them had any idea that it existed! Tons of direct mail and commercials all went completely unnoticed. This little fact is something that the organization obviously needed to hear as painful as it was. The discussion progressed to asking the group what the investment division could do to truly bring value to the client base of the bank. The bank staff listened carefully as the focus groups talked about conducting educational sessions on various topics and how the bank had built in credibility on financial issues. They also disclosed that the brand was strong and that educational sessions would be well attended because of that fact. The bank asked group members what topics they felt would be the most well attended sessions and the groups agreed on a couple.

Several focus groups later, nearly 50 higher level banking clients agreed that two topics would be good for educational sessions for people like them. The bank listened. They designed two workshops on the topics involved and let their target market know that the bank was offering them. In addition to the marketing, they called the 50 wealthy clients that said they would find tremendous value in learning about the topics to let them know that they would be conducting the sessions. Many attended. They had to conduct several sessions because they were full. The power of the feedback and knowledge is right there within our own client base.

So many of us spend hours racking our brains about how to improve, how to get more clients, how to get better responses to marketing, and how to brand ourselves better. We hire coaches (like me), attend workshops (like the ones I speak at), and go to conventions (like the ones I attend), yet we never take action on what makes the most sense. We never look within our own client base for the answer to our challenges.

Client Centered Focus Groups will allow you to engage your most respected clients and relationships in a process that is fun, inexpensive, very effective, and can have a significant impact on the way you provide your service. Your clients are typically the people who trust you the most. They are eager to help; we rarely give them the platform or an organized way to do so. Client Centered Focus Groups allow you to engage your most valuable assets in your business and learn from them in an environment that they appreciate and respect. There are many challenges that we all face as business owners that focus groups can help us solve. Below are some of the most popular among my clients.

How Do I Improve the Retention of Our Clients?

All the marketing in the world will not help a company that is losing clients more quickly than they gain them. You would be amazed at how many corporations hire me to come into their companies to conduct focus groups for prospects, not current clients. When I ask them if all of their clients use all of their services and if their retention is as good as it can be they look confused. Invariably the answer to that question is, "I don't know?" Until that question is answered, focus groups with prospects (next section) should not be implemented. You must first maximize the opportunity within your own client base. Client retention and satisfaction is number one.

Conducting Client Centered Focus Groups will help any organization identify service issues that may be hurting retention. What is really amazing is that those clients who give feedback during the focus group about service issues were probably future "past" clients but the focus group allowed them the forum to talk about things that can be improved. There are so many benefits to this one tool. Improving client retention is a big one.

How Do I Promote New Products or Services to My Clients?

Most organizations continue to add to the value they offer their client base. They evolve as times goes on through acquisitions and partnerships, changing industries and product changes, and they continue to market additional services to their clients. Many of my clients are disappointed that more of their clients don't take advantage of their additional products and services. The bank mentioned above is a perfect example. My first question to my clients is; "Do they understand that these products and services are available and what the benefits are?" Most of the time, you know the answer to that question; "I don't know?" It is quite easy to go find out.

Client Centered Focus Groups can be an excellent way to introduce a targeted group of existing clients to a service that your organization has added to bring value to them. The groups allow you to tell the focus group that you had added the services to bring value to your client base but had not tested if the clients actually saw the value. The focus group is simply a good format to present the products or services and gain honest feedback on the value of them, and if there are objections. The secondary benefit is that you are thoroughly educating the same people you are trying to market the products and services to. Gaining new users of your products and services is a natural benefit of conducting the groups. If you are introducing new products or services, let the people you are marketing them to tell you the best way to approach them.

How Do I Duplicate My Top Clients Through Referral?

This is a similar purpose to many Client Interactive Surveys. To create clients that are compelled to talk to other people about you, you first have to assess how they value and view your service. Do they understand your business and your service? Do they understand who the target market of your business is? What service issues may exist that stop clients from referring business? How do clients want to be approached about growing your business? These are all questions that only they can answer.

Client Centered Focus Groups are an excellent way to clarify what you are trying to accomplish to a captive group of top clients and then gain their advice on your service and how to accomplish your growth objectives. If they see you as a business with business challenges, they are happy to help. Many people have Advisory Councils comprised of top clients. While the intent of these groups is good, I believe there is a better way. Most of the people that I work with say that their Advisory Council is limited. A small group of people who meet to discuss ideas and give feedback to the business executive is a good thing to have, but you frequently run out of things to talk about with one small group. Client Centered Focus Groups will accomplish that same objective but with a much broader base of clients. You are unlimited as far as the number of groups that you can do.

Don't listen to me tell you how to get more referrals from your top clients. Listen to your top clients tell you how to get more people like them. That is like me asking some random women from another city who doesn't know my wife the key to making her happy? Wouldn't it be more effective to just explain to my wife that I want her to be happy and want to ask her some questions on how to accomplish that objective? The answer was simple by the way, shopping.

There are hundreds of other reasons to use focus groups. You can improve employee morale, become more effective at recruiting to your company, learn what your competition does that you don't, understand how the public perceives your brand, and pretty much anything else you want to know.

Now, those of you who are marketing gurus and work for marketing research firms have probably already burned this book. They hate the idea that I say you can do your own focus groups. They will tell you that you won't get honest feedback and that people won't be objective with you. They will tell you that only by hiring a third party can you truly execute a focus group that will drive results. Those comments come from people who charge $20,000 to come in and conduct one. The reality is that I have owned some big companies and some small companies. The people reading this may not be in the position to spend $100,000 this year on market research that they could have done themselves. If you do have that kind of budget, contact me.

If you honestly want to improve your business and solve your challenges, your focus groups will help you in that effort. They will be honest with you and shoot you straight if they can tell that you are there for that purpose. Client Centered Focus Groups are an incredible tool to use with your best relationships. Showing your clients and best relationships how much you respect their input and opinions is a valuable gesture.

The following pages will be a step by step guide to conducting Client Centered Focus Groups. These groups are also very effective at being more attractive to prospects but that will come in the following section. Again, before you worry about being more valuable to prospects, make sure that you are valuable to your clients. There is no point in pouring water into a bottomless bucket no matter how much you enjoy frustration.

You will notice that the steps to implementing this process are remarkably similar to the steps to implementing Interactive Client Surveys. That is the simplicity of the Feedback Marketing System. When you master one of these skills, you can master them all. There are very real differences in the two approaches that will be important to learn so don't let the similarity convince you that the pages aren't worth the read. The success is in the details.

Step 1 – Identify What Your Challenges Are

Much like Interactive Client Surveys, this process begins by identifying the current challenges in your business and writing them down. Obviously, there are certain challenges that focus groups cannot help you solve. Write down a list of the most pressing challenges you face. Sometimes, you will have many different challenges — they can't all be addressed in a focus group. You will have to identify the most pressing issue in your business.

Writing down the challenges will help you identify who will be best at helping find solutions. I always ask my clients to list the things that they feel are stopping them from achieving the level that they would like to achieve. An example may be:

The biggest challenges that I currently face in my business are:

1. *I am not sure that my best clients really understand the services that we offer.*

2. *I am not sure if my clients really see the value in all of the services that we offer.*

3. *I am unclear as to whether or not my current clients know that I want to grow my business and what kind of clients I want to recruit.*

4. *My clients have not taken advantage of new services.*

5. *I do not consistently receive quality referrals from my existing clients.*

As you can see, these challenges somewhat relate to one another. Many times you will find that a lot of your challenges stem from your clients not really having a firm grasp on the services that you offer. Moreover, they are often unaware that they can play an active role in helping you execute that plan. Not having an understanding that you want to grow your business, who you want to grow the business with, and what they have to do with that obviously will impact the number and kind of referrals. Regardless of the challenges you face, you must write them down so that you can develop your purpose for conducting Client Centered Focus Groups. You must be able to clearly articulate to your respected clients what those challenges are, why you feel focus groups can help you overcome those challenges, and what you have enlisted their support to resolve. While each of these aspects will be discussed in detail in the coming pages, the next step is to begin developing your purpose statement and your key objectives.

NOTE: In the first section I used the financial services field for my examples of structuring Interactive Client Surveys. For purposes of diversity, I will use a large executive coaching firm in the coming pages. This firm has hundreds of coaches throughout the country who focus their coaching services on business owners and addressing the common challenges that business owners face. This will show you the diversity of the approaches we are discussing.

Step 2 – Write Your Purpose Statement and Objectives

If there is one area where I see professionals and organizations take short cuts, it is in this phase of development. Taking a short cut here will lead to limited effectiveness in this entire process. As you will see, your purpose statement and objectives serve a much greater purpose than documenting what you want to accomplish. The key to effectively implementing Client Centered Focus Groups is in having a genuine purpose and clear cut objectives. Beyond just having an idea of what you want to accomplish, you will see that the foundation for many steps in this process will require that you have clearly defined your purpose and objectives. This step will be critical in:

Developing Your Structure

Much like Interactive Client Surveys, Client Centered Focus Groups will require you to clearly develop the structure for the time that you are in front of the participants. You will find that when you begin your Introduction, you will need to refer back to your challenges and what compelled you to develop focus groups. You will also refer to your clear cut objectives on an agenda that will be in front of the group. Your discussion questions and your questionnaire questions will be based on those objectives and geared toward accomplishing them. As you can see, every piece of the focus group will require that you have written a purpose statement and defined your objectives.

Filling Up the Room

The invitation process for the Client Centered Focus Group is a bit different in that you will not be asking your clients to come in for a one-to-one meeting. You will need to explain why you are conducting focus groups and what you hope to accomplish. You will see that the foundation of this invitation language will be in your purpose statement and objectives. You will also find that you are often face to face with someone who is a potential participant for one of your groups. When that is the case, you cannot just say, "Will you attend a focus group?" You need to explain why you are conducting groups and what you want to accomplish. Again, the foundation of the entire process is this step.

You will want to write a paragraph or two giving a summary of the overall purpose of the focus group and an overall objective that you would like to accomplish. You will then want to break your objectives into smaller, more specific steps that will later be used to develop your questionnaire. As we discussed earlier, I will use the example of an executive coaching firm with whom I worked. They had developed a process that could help larger business owners become more effective in their day to day activities. When implemented, they believed that their process would dramatically increase the bottom line for the business owner and thus rationalize large fees for the coaching process.

As you will hear me say many times, it doesn't matter what the executive coaching firm thinks, it matters what the business owners that they will target with their process will think. As a means of figuring that out, they decided to look internally at their existing clients. Many of these clients were in fact large business owners that had never seen the process that was developed. It was relatively new and thus had not been "rolled out" to the current clients. A natural place for them to begin was to inquire with their current clients who fit their target market to learn what they thought of the value of the process and how to market it. Below is an example of their Purpose Statement and their objectives.

Our firm has worked to develop a solution for large business owners that will increase their bottom line profits through a series of assessments and adjustments. While we feel that we have a good understanding of the challenges that these business owners face and how our process can solve those challenges, we want to explore what our target clients think of those two key issues before we spend our resources promoting the process. We want to conduct Client Centered Focus Groups to present what we have developed to a targeted audience and assess their response to what was developed. This will help us make adjustments prior to marketing the process. Specifically, our objectives will be:

1. *To present our consulting process to a captive audience of 6-8 large business owner clients.*

2. *To gain feedback on our perception of our target client and the challenges they face.*

3. *To learn what our target audience identifies as their main challenge that has not been addressed.*

4. *To gain feedback on the primary value that our process delivers and what their perception of the monetary value is of the service.*

5. *To define the objections that business owners would have to going through the process and implementing it in their business models.*

6. *To learn how to approach the target audience in a way that is consistent with their challenges and the solutions that we want to provide.*

As you can see, these objectives are very well defined. You will later see how this purpose statement and those objectives are re-iterated through the invitation language that they used and the questionnaires that they developed. They essentially want to get their target audience in a room and present it to them in a setting that promotes honesty. The executive coaching firm was intelligent enough to know that they could go out and meet one-on-one with business owners and present the process, but, they would never really know what was going on in the minds of the business owners as they presented. This format will tell them.

After clearly documenting the challenges that you face in your business model, the purpose statement and objective should come naturally. You should simply have a very clearly defined list of challenges along with what population of your current clients or relationships will be helpful in solving them. Your purpose statement and objectives will clearly outline what you want to solve. The next step in the process is to select the clients that you want to ask to participate.

Step 3 – Selecting Your Clients

Selecting your clients should be a very well thought out process. I encourage my clients to begin with a complete list of current clients and relationships. Much like Interactive Client Surveys I encourage them to begin by asking one question about each of the people on the list; "If I had 100 of this type of client, what would my business look like?"

Some of us are tempted to add people to the list just because they are wealthy or they employ a lot of people who could be potential clients; however, ignore the fact that we don't really like them as people or have respect for the way they conduct themselves. If you feel that way when you look at a name, I would encourage you to keep them off of your list. While they may have a lot of money, chances are that they don't have the influence that you think they might. If you don't respect them, there is a good chance that many of their clients and employees don't either.

The main difference between Interactive Client Surveys and Client Centered Focus Groups is that you have to add a second layer to your focus group selection process that you do not have to do with a one-to-one setting.

We all know that there are certain types of people who are not good in group settings. You have to think of the personality styles on your list after you have implemented the Rule of 100. You will find that there are different types of personalities on your list. You will realize that there are some people on your list who are chronically negative. They are never happy with anything. Get them off your list. You will realize that there are people who are very dominating and never let anyone get a word in edgewise. Get them off your list as well. You will have some wall flowers who you know would be scared to death in a focus group. Get them off the list. Your list should be comprised of people that you know are social people and a good fit for the topic that you want to talk about.

When many of my clients are going through the client selection process, they say they have some names that they are on the fence about. They may feel that they would not blend with the group or may be too negative. The only thing that I can tell you is to trust your judgment. If you feel like there may be a problem with someone when you look at their name, there will more than likely be a problem. You don't want the entire group to suffer because you let someone with a very unusual personality come into the group and hinder the progress you want to make.

This is one of the primary reasons that I recommend that my clients do both Client Centered Focus Groups and Interactive Client Surveys. You can segment the lists so that you have a group of people who would be right for focus groups, and a list of people who would be better for one-to-one meetings. That way, you get a variety of opinions and feedback without leaving people out because of personality issues.

Some people look at their client list and feel like they may not have enough quality clients to do a focus group. If you are in this position, don't force it. You should look at starting with Interactive Client Surveys and probably even broaden that to include surveying some people who are not clients but will talk to you. Don't put random groups of people together just so you can have a focus group. Nothing is more uncomfortable than having a group of completely different people trying to give opinions on something that may not even be relevant to them.

In the example of the executive coaching firm, imagine if they did not have enough business owners who met their target criterion so they let people who were employees attend. Would employees really have input into the minds of the business owners? You should never compromise quality for quantity in a focus group. I have often said that Ford Motor Company would not allow you into a focus group if you do not have a driver's license. They could not afford to make marketing decisions based on feedback from the wrong populations. You are no different. Make sure your list is a good one.

You will want to insure that after the selection process you are left with a list of at least 25 potential participants. This will allow you to fill up a minimum of two focus groups. When they are prospective clients that number will go up as you don't get nearly as many prospects to participate as you should clients. Clients are normally happy to help out in any way that they can. I am often asked, what is the incentive for them to give me the time? While you can compensate current clients for their time in the form of a gift card, I find that you normally do not need to. There are some more details on this in the coming sections; however, most of your clients will be happy to come in and help in any way that they can.

After you have identified the challenges you want to solve, the purpose and objectives of the group, and the potential participants for the group, you need to begin to structure the time that you will be spending in the focus groups. You will see that structure in these groups is the key to success.

Step 4 – Structuring the Group

Once you have clearly detailed your purpose statement and your objectives, you need to begin putting structure to the group. I recommend that you follow a similar structure to your Interactive Client Surveys. In fact, you will see that each component of Client Centered Focus Groups is the same; the details within each component will change slightly. The focus group that you develop will more than likely have an Introduction, a Presentation, a Discussion, and a Questionnaire. Some of my clients actually use some of the things that they originally developed for their Interactive Client Surveys in their Client Centered Focus Groups. You will see the similarities throughout this section. To begin, I recommend that you document your Introduction.

Introduction

The Introduction in a Client Centered Focus Group occurs when the conductor sits down in front of the group, and begins to give them an overall summary of the group. This Introduction should include three key components:
- Why did we decide to do focus groups
- What key objectives do we want to accomplish
- What will occur during the focus group

The Introduction will normally consume the first four to five minutes and has a much greater purpose than just being the introduction to the group. When people participate in focus groups, they have typically agreed to do so over the phone or in person upon the request of the person or firm conducting the group. There are many different reasons that people attend these groups. It is in most people's nature to want to be helpful. It is also in their nature to want to feel as though they are contributing to something. They like the idea that they were 'selected' from a group and that their opinions are important. In this situation, because they are your clients or relationships, they should also have some connection with you and desire to give back to you.

Even though they have agreed to participate in the group, many will not remember what you are conducting the groups to accomplish or why you are doing them. They are also typically uncertain as to what will occur over the hour and what role they are expected to play. Through developing a structured Introduction to the focus group, you can get everyone in the room comfortable with what they have committed to and what will be expected of them. It will take inactive and reserved people and make them active participants. In the situation with our executive consulting firm, I have provided the example of a quality Introduction below.

On behalf of ABC Executive Consulting, I want to thank you all for agreeing to participate. My name is Dan Allison, which most of you already knew, and I will be conducting the focus group today. I want to begin the group by explaining why we decided to conduct these focus groups, what our primary objectives are with the focus groups, and what will occur over the hour that we have asked of you.

Why Did We Decide to Do Focus Groups?

We have operated an executive consulting firm for just short of two decades. During that time we have had the pleasure of becoming highly involved with business owners throughout the country. We have continued to see many our clients and business owners who may not use our services struggle with some very pressing issues that we did not have a solution for.

We focused most of our efforts on the consulting model that we had developed and stayed within our niche.

A few years ago, we began to look at the challenges facing business owners to identify what organizations were in place to help business owners address them. We were not able to consistently find these solutions for business owners. We began at that time developing a full consulting model designed specifically to help them with the challenges that we have previously not engaged in.

We concluded the development of this platform early this year. We are now in the phase of rolling it out to the marketplace and marketing the process to prospective business owners. As we considered our marketing plans, we realized that we currently served many of the business owners that we designed this process for, and we had not received an honest critique of what we have developed.

What Key Objectives Do We Want to Accomplish?

We decided that a natural next step would be to conduct a few focus groups to gain the insight and expertise of clients who have trusted us with other areas of their business. We felt that conducting a few focus groups would help us understand how well we have identified the challenges that we set out to solve and how well our solution will solve them. We are using a series of these focus groups to accomplish the following objectives referred to on your agendas (covered later):

1. To gain feedback on our perception of our target client and the challenges they face.

2. To learn what our target audience identifies as their main challenge that has not been addressed.

83

3. *To gain feedback on the primary value that our process delivers and what their perception of the monetary value is of the service.*

4. *To define the objections that business owners would have to going through the process and implementing it in their business models.*

5. *To learn how to approach the target audience in a way that is consistent with their challenges and the solutions that we want to provide.*

We appreciate your involvement in this group and have asked you to be involved because of the high level of respect we have for everyone in the room.

What Will Occur During the Focus Group?

Over the hour, we have a structured agenda as you can see. We first plan to give an overview of the service that we designed. We will give you an overview of what challenges we perceived business owners facing and what solutions we designed to solve them. After the 20 minute overview, we will move on to a 20-25 minute discussion. We have prepared a few questions that we would like to ask very directly and get the feedback we know we will not get out in the field. Toward the end, we have a brief questionnaire to get a little more feedback that we will not get to in the discussion. We have some food that will be brought in at the end so that we don't get distracted during the discussion. If you need to get back to the office, please feel free to box up some food and get going. If you have additional comments or questions, certainly feel free to stick around and eat some food here.

As you can see, the sample Introduction is very straightforward, however; it is also very methodical and structured. You have to be able to articulate those three key aspects of the focus group to insure that everyone understands your rationale, your objectives, and what they have to do with all of this. This is especially critical when they are prospective clients and may not have a high level of trust for you.

However you decide to communicate your Introduction, it should be structured with those three key components. You can be as detailed as you would like within those three, but don't stray from that structure. If you do, you will immediately notice that your participants feel distant and not ready to participate. This will be because you have done a poor job of communicating purpose and objectives. This is one of the most critical aspects of conducting Client Centered Focus Groups; clear expectations and goals.

After developing your Introduction and how you will begin your Client Centered Focus Groups, you will move into presenting the content that you want to gain feedback on. Like every other piece of the group, it should be well thought out and structured.

The Presentation

While focus groups can be very open ended and more focused on getting feedback from participants on very general topics, most of the time a focus group will involve a presentation of some sort. You do not necessarily need to give a formal power point style presentation; however, you will typically need to structure a presentation of some sort to get the feedback that you want to get.

After giving a five minute Introduction covering your purpose and objectives for the Client Centered Focus Group, you will be able to give a 20-25 minute presentation to the group. The topic of the presentation should be focused on what you want to gain feedback on. For some people, that may be the presentation of a product that they want to promote to their client base. For others, it may be a process or strategy that they plan to promote to the client base. Many times it is a presentation of the business model in general and the main objectives for the business heading into the future. You can present anything that you want to get honest feedback on.

If you have struggled to market a product or service to your existing client base, these focus groups are an excellent way to present the product or service to a captive group of targeted clients and learn why you have struggled with getting clients to engage.

A Client Centered Focus Group will help you understand if the products or services are desirable, or if they don't have the value that you thought they did. You may find out that your products or services have incredible value, but the way you are marketing them is not effective.

I have saved hundreds of thousands of dollars in marketing money that would have been ineffectively spent because focus groups critiqued the marketing strategy that I was going to employ. Still other times I learned that it was not a marketing issue, it was a service or product issue. I learned that no matter how well I marketed a product or service, it was not as valuable to the target consumer as I thought it would be. I learned to price things higher and I learned to price things lower. One of the great benefits of conducting Client Centered Focus Groups is that it is also an incredibly effective marketing tool in itself. Think about it, in what other setting can you present your product or service to a captive group of your targeted consumer as they listen intently and take notes? If your product or service is extremely valuable, you will gain new clients from your presentation.

It is critical to note here that this cannot be the primary motivation for conducting Client Centered Focus Groups. If you use focus groups as a "clever" way to fill a room and market to people without giving the feedback the emphasis it needs, they will completely backfire on you. They cannot be used as a time share scam. I want to repeat that as it is one of the most important things I will mention in this book, they cannot be used to close people for business. I do have to acknowledge that people may become users of the product or service as a result of being exposed to it through the focus group, but that should be a natural secondary benefit to doing them.

If your content requires more than 20-25 minutes to present, you should first consider whether or not you are presenting too much information. Most products or services can very clearly be presented or demonstrated in that period of time. If you have to extend that time frame, I would extend the focus group accordingly. It is critical that you have more time in discussion that you do presenting. The group should talk more than you do for it to be an effective focus group.

With current clients, you may also just want to get feedback on their experience with your firm. You may want to know what things they value and what things you may be able to improve on. You may want to ask them what the most effective way to expand on your service would be. You may want to learn how to approach your current client base about the topic of referrals. All of these things can be accomplished through a Client Centered Focus Group. You just have to structure some form of presentation to give your existing clients a feel for where your business is currently at and where you want to take it. They can then give you their feedback on how to most effectively get there.

If you have advisory boards or boards of directors, think of this as a much more versatile version of that. When I owned mental health clinics, we had Governing Boards of public officials, highly educated psychologist and psychiatrists, and all of the experts you could need to get great advice. Their feedback rarely compared to the feedback directly from my customers. You learn the most from your customers; however, most of us don't give them a good format to teach us. At best we do surveys and everyone knows how I feel about mailed surveys.

In the example of our executive coaching firm and their focus groups with business owner clients, their presentation involved a 20 minute overview of the new consulting platform they developed. They gave a power point presentation covering the needs that they saw business owners having and how their new platform was designed to solve those needs. I often tell my clients who want feedback on a product or service to pretend that the participants have given you the opportunity to come in there and pitch them the features and benefits of your product or service. That is the presentation that you should give.

It is important to note however, that you should remove the salesmanship from a focus group presentation. It has to be an objective presentation of the content. If you jump up and down with passion while presenting your products the participants will realize that you are already convinced that you have it all figured out and will not give you the feedback that you want. Give a clear, objective presentation on the product or service and what you perceive the value to be to the consumer. Then, simply develop questions to explore how well you have identified the challenges the clients face and how well the solution addresses those challenges.

You will want to test the presentation for time. Many professionals feel comfortable in groups of people and assume that they will just wing the presentation of content. If you do this, chances are you will run over on time and compromise some of the feedback time. This is a critical mistake as you want to insure that the majority of the time is spent interacting.

At this point, you will have a five minute Introduction prepared along with no more than a 25 minute presentation. The next step is to develop the second half of the focus group. This is the most enjoyable part of the group because it is the part where the clients actually talk. The first thing to develop will be the discussion questions to get feedback on the content that you presented.

Discussion

After developing your presentation of content and testing it to insure that it falls within the time frame that you have allotted, you will need to develop your questions for the group to discuss. Focus group discussion questions are primarily going to be open ended questions that are a bit general. The main focus of these questions should be on the content that was presented. Most professionals want to identify if the clients see the need for the product or service, and how well it solves the problems that the clients have. There are thousands of different questions that can be asked.

I recommend that you have roughly four to five open ended questions developed. The discussion will last a minimum of 20 minutes and most groups cannot get through more questions than that. That is why the questionnaire is an important supplement to the feedback. The focus group discussion questions should be the most pressing questions that you have for the group to answer. They should be the questions that can help you solve the challenges that you face and should resemble the objectives that you developed for the focus group. Some example questions would be:

- What do you see as the primary challenges that this population faces?

- What do you feel is the most valuable component of the product or service that was presented?
- What do you feel the major drawback is of the product or service that was presented?
- What do you feel the price point should be for the product or service that was discussed?
- If you were in our position and wanted to further promote this product or service to our client base, what kinds of marketing would you do for it?
- How do you feel this product or service impacts the likelihood that our clients will refer us to other people like them?

Your questions should be intentionally direct. Again, a marketing research firm would tell you that you cannot get honest feedback on questions like these; however, I have coached thousands of people on this process as well as conducted many groups myself and can tell you that this is not the case. When the participants can tell that you genuinely want their help in solving a problem or assessing content or the value of your services, they will be absolutely honest and direct with you. Just ask any questions that you have.

In the example of our executive coaching firm doing focus groups with current clients who own a large business, they had very well defined objectives. They wanted to learn if their perception of the main challenges facing business owners was accurate. They wanted to see if they had indeed developed a solution that business owners would be likely to respond to. And, they wanted to know what improvements could be made to the consulting platform to insure that it was as valuable as possible. Therefore, these were their four discussion questions:

- When we explained our perception of the most common challenges that business owners are facing, which challenges do you feel are accurate and what you do feel is the most pressing challenge facing business owners?
- What component of the consulting platform that we presented do you feel stood out as being the most valuable?
- What was the main drawback to the platform that we developed and what do you see as the main objection a business owner would have to going through the process?

- If you wanted to effectively promote this process to business owners, what activities would you do to market it?

While these questions are very simple and straightforward, they were able to learn a great deal about the key selling points of the process. They were able to better understand the pain that business owners experience and how their platform addresses those pain points. They learned that their price point was on the high side and would likely be a major objection. Finally, they were introduced through one of the focus group participants to a large meeting of business owners to present the process and gain additional feedback.

Discussion questions will naturally evolve into additional questions. It is easy to fill 20-25 minutes discussing just one of the questions. That is why you really need to assess the timeframe of your focus group. While an hour is typical, you may need to extend that time frame a bit to insure that you get to all of the questions. Again, you have to keep the time in mind because you don't want to get wrapped up in a question and not get to the three critical questions. I tell all of my clients to imagine that they have a boss who has promised to fire them if they walk out of the meeting with any of the questions unanswered. You have to keep the discussion moving. We will talk about the technique to do so in later sections.

If you are nervous that you may not be able to fill the discussion time you can have back up questions prepared. I can tell you from a lot of experience that people will talk a lot more than you think they will. These people are very aware that they are coming to a focus group and are expected to talk. They will not be shy once they have begun talking. You will want to make sure that you plan your questions accordingly.

Questionnaire

After developing your discussion questions, you will want to move on to developing additional questions for a questionnaire. The questionnaire is typically completed during the last ten minutes of the focus group. Unlike the discussion, these questions can also be rating scale questions. I definitely recommend that you put many open ended questions on the questionnaire as well, but rating scale questions are a great compliment.

Rating scale questions are typically designed to assess how strongly someone feels about something. Open ended questions will tell you why they feel the way they do. An example of an open ended question would be:

- *What do you see as the primary value of the product or service that was presented?*

A rating scale question may ask:

- *On a scale of 1 to 10, how well do you feel that this product or service addresses the needs that our customers have?*

1 2 3 4 5 6 7 8 9 10
Not Well   Fairly Well   Extremely Well

As you can see, the rating scale will tell you how valuable the client thinks the product or service is, but the open ended question will tell you what about the product or service is valuable. They are both very important aspects to promoting a product or a service.

I recommend that you give participants one to two minutes per open ended question. If you plan to give them ten minutes to complete a questionnaire, you will need to insure that you don't place more than 5 open ended questions on the questionnaire. Rating scale questions are much easier to complete and they will be able to answer several per minute. They are designed to get an immediate reaction rather than open ended questions which require a little more thought.

I typically develop about ten questions per questionnaire. Don't get fixated on the number of questions that you have on the questionnaire. Never compromise quality for quantity. Of the ten questions I typically develop, five are open ended and about five will be rating scale questions. On the following page, I have provided the complete questionnaire that was used by the executive coaching firm conducting focus groups with current business owner clients.

Name _____

Date of Focus Group _____

We want to thank you for your participation in our focus group. You have been asked to participate because we value and respect your input and feedback. This questionnaire is designed to gain additional feedback on questions that are vital to our growth and providing the level of service we desire to provide to our clients. We sincerely appreciate your thorough and honest answers to these questions. The answers will be used to help us provide an exceptional experience to our valued clients.

1. Do you feel that business owners take the time to address the key issues that we addressed? If not, what do you feel stops them from covering such important issues?

2. What do you feel is the most valuable aspect of the consulting platform discussed?

3. On a scale of 1 to 10, how well do you feel the consulting platform discussed would address the main challenges business owners face?

1 2 3 4 5 6 7 8 9 1 0
Not Well   Fairly Well   Very Well

4. What do you feel would be the biggest drawback or objection a business owner would have to using this service?

5. What do you think the appropriate price point is for the first year of this service?

6. As a business owner, what advice would you give us to make this process more desirable?

7. On a scale of 1 to 10, how likely would you be to recommend a process like this to other business owners?

1 2 3 4 5 6 7 8 9 1 0
Not Likely   Somewhat Likely   Very Likely

As you can see, the answers to these questions were invaluable to learning how business owners would perceive the process that the executive coaching firm wanted to promote. In the process, they were also able to learn if their current clients would be likely to use the platform.

After taking the time to carefully design the questionnaire, you will have each component of your Client Centered Focus Group prepared. You have written your Introduction, and designed a presentation and discussion questions to gain feedback. The questionnaire completes the structure. Now it is time to fill up the focus group.

Step 5 – Filling the Room

At this point in your process, you will know why you are doing focus groups and what you want to accomplish. You have also identified which clients you would like to participate in the groups and what will occur during the time that you have asked of them. The next step is to schedule the focus group date and begin filling up the room.

For a Client Centered Focus Group you will typically want between 6-10 participants. I like to keep it right around 8 participants. This is enough that you get a variety of participants and small enough that nobody falls through the cracks during the discussion.

I recommend that all focus group participants either be invited via telephone or personal invitation. I never recommend mailing an invitation. Mailing invitations feels much less personal. It is difficult for your clients to believe that they were specifically selected for a focus group when you mail the invitation. This is a highly personal and selective process and should feel that way. On that note, the invitation should not be outsourced to an assistant. If these clients are important to you and your business, you should personally pick up the phone and invite them to attend.

While most of your clients would be happy to attend whatever you ask them to attend, it is still important to structure your invitation script so that they have a clear idea of what they are agreeing to. Much like Interactive Client Surveys, the clients need to know that they are coming in specifically to talk about your business and help you solve a challenge through giving their feedback. You have to insure that they understand they are coming into a group and will be expected to talk. If they are hesitant about the group setting, remember that you can do one-to-one meetings as well. That is the main reason I recommend that you do both Interactive Client Surveys and Client Centered Focus Groups. Not everyone is a good fit for the focus group process.

The invitation script will be broken into two parts. Again, when someone answers the phone, they are not actively listening. You need to design an introductory paragraph that will change that. You will need to give them a brief overview of why you are calling and ask if they have a moment for you to explain. The executive coaching firm conducting Client Centered Focus Groups with current clients who owned a business used the following script:

Hey Bill, this is Dan Allison with ABC Executive Coaching, how are you? Great, I was calling because our firm is going to be conducting a few small focus groups with a very select population of our current client base. You are one of the people that we specifically wanted to approach to see if you would be part of one of our groups. Do you have a minute for me to explain what I am asking you to be part of?

Thanks, as you know, our firm continues to evolve and change as our clients do. Over the last three years, we have been developing a new consulting platform designed for business owners. We are prepared to launch the service but would like to gain a little bit of feedback from current clients prior to doing so. We want to insure that we are addressing the right issues, presenting it in a compelling way, and pricing it right. I have a high level of respect for your experience and insight. Would you be part of a group of 6-8 current business owner clients to come in and give us your input?

Again, it may seem lengthy when you could just ask them to come in, but, it is important to clearly explain why you are doing them and what you want to accomplish. It helps them understand that they were specifically selected and that you respect their opinions. It never hurts to flatter one of your top clients by telling them that you respect them enough to get their feedback on critical issues. With current clients, your invitation process should be very easy and you should gain participation from a large majority of them. If not, you should be doing some focus groups to find out how to improve your relationships with your current clients.

I recommend that you confirm 9 to 10 participants for your Client Centered Focus Group. Most of the time, you will have a client or two who is unable to honor the commitment that they have made. I recommend that someone from your office always call to confirm attendance roughly 48 hours prior to the focus group. I recommend that you use the following script:

Hello Bill, this is Dan Allison with ABC Executive Coaching. I was calling to confirm that I have you down for one of the eight spots for our upcoming focus group on Friday, July 9th. If for any reason you are unable to honor that commitment, please give us a call back so that we can fill the spot from our back up list. We will look forward to seeing you at 5:30 p.m on that date. If you have any questions prior to the group, please contact me at 402-350-2532.

The script for confirmation is important because you want to insure that they understand that they have made a commitment and if they don't show up, it will be noticed. When you explain that there are a limited number of slots and that they are taking one up it insures that they will at least call if they are unable to attend. You do not want to wonder how many will show up ten minutes prior to the focus group starting. Some of my clients also like to send confirmation letters. These letters confirm the date, time and location. They also serve as a thank you for their participation. A sample confirmation letter would read:

Dear Bill,

I want to sincerely thank you for agreeing to participate in our upcoming focus group. As we discussed on the phone, I plan to use this feedback from a select group of my clients to give all of my clients the best experience possible. I have some very specific questions that will help us get the feedback from participants and am certainly glad that you have agreed to share your thoughts with our group.

As a reminder, the focus group will be held on July 9th, 2010 from 11:30a-12:30p. We ask that everyone arrive a few minutes early out of respect for everyone's time. We will hold the focus group at The Ivey which is located at XXXXXXXXXX. We will serve food and refreshments to the group.

We have only reserved 8 spots for this focus group so if something should come up, please let us know at your earliest convenience so that we may work from our back up list. Again, thanks so much for agreeing to participate. I will look forward to seeing you and receiving the feedback you will offer the group.

Respectfully,

Dan Allison
ABC Executive Coaching
President

Between sending the letter and placing outbound confirmation calls, you should have a high level of participation amongst your clients who have committed. The next step in the process is to insure that you have set the appropriate environment for the group.

Step 6 – Setting the Stage

It is important to insure that from the moment people arrive until the moment they depart from your Client Centered Focus Group, you have structured an environment that is conducive to what you want to accomplish. This involves insuring that you have a professional environment that is free of distractions and all of your material in place prior to your attendees arriving.

The Environment

It is important to remember that these events are not to be confused with client appreciation events. Some of my clients are inclined to think that these Client Centered Focus Groups should occur in a nice restaurant setting. The opposite is actually true. You want to insure that you secure a private location that is preferably in an office setting. An ideal place for a focus group is a conference room that is suitable for 10-12 people. The more you control the environment, the better you will be.

If your offices don't have an environment that is conducive to a private conference room setting for 10-12 people, you should think about the professional network that you have and who may have an environment that you can use. It is important that the environment say that you are there to work, not to entertain. These focus groups are about accomplishing objectives in a relatively small period of time. This means that you have to have very few distractions. If you don't have a professional network to work with, you may want to consider local libraries or universities. They often have rooms that are set up for this kind of environment.

One word of caution is to avoid restaurants at all cost. You will spend way too much time and money and at the end of the day will accomplish half of what you want to because of ordering, interruptions, and small talk that will occur naturally in this type of a social environment.

Within the private conference style room that you have selected, you will want to insure that you have a table that will comfortably seat 10-12 in a U shape or in a circle. You should never arrange the room classroom style. That style psychologically says that they are there to learn, and you are there to teach. The U shape or circle will show that you are there to interact and discuss.

If you can, you should select a room that has some windows as it can feel a bit tight in conference rooms that have no windows. This is not a necessity but it is nice. You will also want to insure that the temperature in the room is comfortable.

The Materials

You will want to prepare a folder with the materials for participants in advance so that everything is orderly. The first thing that you will want to place in the folder is an agenda. The agenda will look much like the agenda for an Interactive Client Survey. You should break it down into the key sections of the focus group. You should show the Introduction and list the objectives, the presentation of content, and the discussion and questionnaire time frames. An example agenda for the executive coaching firm we have been discussing is on the next page.

AGENDA FOR CLIENT CENTERED FOCUS GROUP
DATE

5:30-5:35 p.m.   INTRODUCTION AND OVERVIEW OF KEY
OBJECTIVES

-What lead us to conduct these groups?
-What will happen over the course of the hour?
-Covering our key objectives:

1. *To gain feedback on our perception of our target client and the challenges they face.*

2. *To learn what our target audience identifies as their main challenge that has not been addressed.*

3. *To gain feedback on the primary value that our process delivers and what their perception of the monetary value is of the service.*

4. *To define the objections that business owners would have to going through the process and implementing it in their business models.*

5. *To learn how to approach the target audience in a way that is consistent with their challenges and the solutions that we want to provide.*

5:35-5:55 p.m.   OVERVIEW OF SERVICE

5:55-6:20 p.m.   DISCUSSION ON CORE FIVE QUESTIONS

6:20-6:30 p.m.   COMPLETE FOCUS GROUP
QUESTIONNAIRE

6:30 p.m.   ADJOURN

Thank you for your participation

The agenda should be the first thing that participants see when they open the folder.

The next thing that should be included in the folder is a copy of the presentation or content that you will be discussing with the group. If you are doing a power point presentation, you can print a copy of it with three slides per page. This will be used for participants to follow along with the presentation and take notes as you discuss the key points of the content. If you don't plan on giving a formal power point presentation but plan to give more of an overview of the business and the future objectives that you have for the business, you may want to simply do a one page outline. You want to insure that you stay on track to cover your key points. If you don't have a structure to follow, you will run the risk of talking too long or not covering everything that you want to cover.

Behind the copy of the presentation or the outline of your content, you want to place a copy of the questionnaire on your letterhead. While this will be completed later, I find it helpful for participants to review the questions as they wait for the group to start. This gives them an idea of what they will be giving feedback on and creates a more actively engaged group. When they know what they are expected to discuss, they will pay more attention to the content.

Also in the folder you will want a name tent for the participant to write their name and place in front of themselves. While you may know all of your clients' names, they will not know each other. During the discussion, it is very helpful for them to be able to refer to each other by name and furthers the relationships and the intimacy of the environment. Name tags are difficult to read and often fall off so I recommend folding strong construction paper in half and using them as name tents.

The only other thing that you may want to give them in the folder would be a copy of an article that you feel may interest the group. This article serves no other purpose than to give them something to read while they wait for the group to start. Some people are not very comfortable socializing with people that they do not know. By placing the article in the folder, they will have something to focus on to insure that they remain comfortable.

At this point, you should have a good feel for why you are conducting the group and a very well thought out structure. You have your guests confirmed, the environment is ready and you have all of the materials organized in the folder. The only thing left to do is to conduct the session.

Step 7 – Conducting the Session

As with anything that you will ever do with business, focus groups will get easier the more that you do them. You will find your comfort zone and you will begin to have your own style. I can only give you the frame work and the structure from my experience; you will need to make these groups your own based on your style. The key to making sure that you get everything that you want from the focus groups and that your participants not only engage but enjoy the groups is to know exactly what will happen from the time they walk in the door until the time that they leave. There are several key stages of conducting the group and it all starts with greeting the participants.

Greeting the Participants

I recommend that whoever will be conducting the focus groups actually meet the guests up front. As these are current clients, they probably will be most familiar and comfortable with you. I recommend that as you greet the guest and thank them for their "participation", you quickly review the contents of the folder. I stress "participation" because that is what you want to continue to reinforce. You don't want to thank them for coming; you want to thank them for agreeing to participate.

If you just thank them and hand them the folder they will go into the room and sit down to begin going through the material in the folder. Because you have not walked them through what is in there they will probably initially wonder why there is a copy of a presentation. They may also begin to fill out the questionnaire even though you have not gone over the material necessary to complete it. Nervous people do strange things. It is important for you to go through the material so that they have a good understanding of what is in the folder. I always say the same thing. I recommend that you say:

Hey Bill, thanks for agreeing to participate in the focus group. Before you go into the room, I want to walk you through what is in this folder really quickly. Up front is a copy of the agenda for tonight. We only have an hour, so we will insure we stay on track. Behind the agenda is a copy of the content that we will be sharing and asking the group for feedback on. Behind that is a questionnaire that we will complete at the end. Please hold off on completing the questionnaire until then. Over on the other side is a name tent so that the participants can refer to each other by name. Finally, I put an article in there that I thought people might enjoy reading as we wait for the group to start. We are expecting 8 participants tonight and will begin just after 5:30 p.m.

Giving this brief explanation lets them know that while there is a presentation in there, it does have a point as it is what you want the feedback on. This is even more important with prospective clients as they don't have the trust in you that your clients will. It also insures that you don't have nervous people filling out questionnaires without any of the information that they will need. Finally, it lets them know how many will be in the group which will make those first few people more comfortable. The first few people are always nervous that there will only be a few of them in the group.

Starting the Focus Group

I always begin just a couple of minutes behind because many people show up at the last minute for these groups. I normally will stop into the room very quickly to let the group know that we are waiting for a couple more people to arrive and will begin in just a few minutes. When the time arrives, you should go in and get seated at the head of the conference room table.

I always recommend that you stay seated the entire focus group. I feel like it is helpful for the group to feel like you are part of the group, not a presenter. When you stand up, you go into presentation mode and may begin doing some of the things that you don't even know that you do when you present to people. Remember, this is an environment that is supposed to be conducive to interaction. If you appear to be on stage that is less likely to happen.

As you sit down, begin with the five minute introduction that you have prepared. In the case of our executive coaching firm, they would begin with:

On behalf of ABC Executive Consulting, I want to thank you all for agreeing to participate. My name is Dan Allison, which most of you already knew, and I will be conducting the focus group today. I want to begin the group by explaining why we decided to conduct these focus groups, what our primary objectives are with the focus groups, and what will occur over the hour that we have asked of you.

Why Did We Decide to Do Focus Groups?

We have operated an executive consulting firm for just short of two decades. During that time we have had the pleasure of becoming highly involved with business owners throughout the country. We have continued to see many our clients and business owners who may not use our services struggle with some very pressing issues that we did not have a solution for. We focused most of our efforts on the consulting model that we had developed and stayed within our niche.

A few years ago, we began to look at the challenges of business owners and tried to identify what organizations were in place to help business owners address them. We were not able to consistently find these solutions for business owners. We began at that time developing a full consulting model designed specifically to help them with the challenges that we had not engaged in previously.

We concluded the development of this platform early this year. We are now in the phase of rolling it out to the marketplace and marketing the process to prospective business owners. As we considered our marketing plans, we realized that we currently served many of the business owners that we designed this process for, and we had not received an honest critique of what we have developed.

What Key Objectives Do We Want to Accomplish?

We decided that a natural next step would be to conduct a few focus groups to gain the insight and expertise of clients who have trusted us with other areas of their business. We felt that conducting a few focus groups would help us understand how well we have identified the challenges that we set out to solve and how our solution connects with business owners. We are using a series of these focus groups to accomplish the following objectives referred to on your agendas:

1. *To gain feedback on our perception of our target client and the challenges they face.*

2. *To learn what our target audience identifies as their main challenge that has not been addressed.*

3. *To gain feedback on the primary value that our process delivers and what their perception of the monetary value is of the service.*

4. *To define the objections that business owners would have to going through the process and implementing it in their business models.*

5. *To learn how to approach the target audience in a way that is consistent with their challenges and the solutions that we want to provide.*

We appreciate your involvement in this group and have asked you to be involved because of the high level of respect we have for everyone in the room.

What Will Occur During the Focus Group?

Over the hour, we have a structured agenda as you can see. We first plan to give an overview of the service that we designed. We will give you an overview of what challenges we perceived business owners facing and what solutions we designed to solve them. After the 20 minute overview, we will move on to a 20-25 minute discussion. We have prepared a few questions that we would like to ask very directly and get the feedback we know we will not get out in the field. Toward the end, we have a brief questionnaire to get a little more feedback that we will not get to in the discussion. We have some food that will be brought in at the end so that we don't get distracted during the discussion. If you need to get back to the office, please feel free to box up some food and get going. If you have additional comments or questions, certainly feel free to stick around and eat some food here. If there are no questions, we will begin by giving an overview of the process that we would like the feedback on.

After the introduction, you will move into your presentation of the content on which you are gathering feedback. Again, the thing to keep in mind is that you should try to give an objective presentation. Try to stay away from using sales language when presenting your process, service, or products. Rather than say things like, "This is one of the great things that this will do for YOU," say, "This is one of the benefits that people experience from using this." Replacing the word YOU will make a big difference in the presentation. Remember, you don't want to sell the people in the room. You want whatever you are presenting to be valuable to the larger demographic that these people represent. Focus your presentation of what the value is to the group of people as a whole, not the people specifically in the room.

As you present your topic, you should notice that people are taking notes and paying close attention to what you are saying. They are aware of what kinds of questions you will be asking the group to discuss after the presentation so they pay much more attention in focus groups than they may in a workshop or a seminar on the exact same topic. As you wrap up your presentation, you will want to transition into the group discussion. This is the point where these groups actually get to be a lot of fun. You can transition by saying something simple like:

That is the content that I wanted to share with a few of these groups, now I want to move into the feedback portion of the group. As I told you at the beginning, I have prepared some questions. It would be helpful if I could receive information on these questions. The first question that I wanted to ask the group to discuss is: We explained our perception of the most common challenges that business owners are facing, which challenges do you feel are accurate and what you do feel is the most pressing challenge facing business owners?

The Discussion

Of all of the different pieces of conducting Client Centered Focus Groups, I believe the discussion causes the most anxiety for my consulting clients. They are normally fearful that nobody will talk or that there will be uncomfortable silence. They are nervous that one person will dominate the discussion or that people will become negative in the group. There is one technique that will eliminate all of these concerns and insure that your discussion involves everybody and flows very comfortably and smoothly. I call this technique Verbal Ping Pong. After you ask your first discussion question, there will be a period of silence. Any time you have controlled the floor in front of a group and then turn the tables and ask them a question, there will be that period of silence. It seems like it lasts for thirty minutes even though it is normally only about five to ten seconds. I eliminate that period of time all together by using what I already know about people to begin the discussion. Before the group even starts, you should pick the person that you will call on to begin the discussion. With current clients, this is very easy because you know the personalities in the room.

Pick the person that you know is a very social person and very comfortable in front of groups. These are always the people that seem full of energy and very happy and jovial. I always have their name written down in front of me when I begin the group so that I can avoid the awkward silence. So, to begin the discussion, I would ask the question and then immediately say, "And to avoid an awkward silence, Bill, would you mind starting off giving your feedback on that question?"

You will never run into a problem doing this. Normally, Bill will gladly lean forward and begin talking. Remember, these people came to a focus group. They knew that they would be the ones talking; they just need you to continue to conduct the session. While Bill is giving his feedback, you will obviously want to actively listen to him. You may even want to jot down some notes if he says something that you want to remember. I always audio record the focus groups. This insures that I can pay attention to the participants of the group. When Bill completes his thoughts, I will begin using the Verbal Ping Pong technique. That is that I will simply restate to Bill what I understood his feedback to be, clarify that I understood him correctly, and then pass the conversation on to someone else. So for example, I will say, "Bill, do I understand that you feel the biggest challenge that a business owner faces is insuring that personal finances and business finances are managed together to insure that they both work in a business owner's favor?" When he confirms that I understood his feedback I will say, "Thanks for that feedback, John, what is your opinion of what Bill said, do you have a similar opinion?"

Do you see how I hit the ball to Bill, he hit it back to me, and then I hit it to John? This is Verbal Ping Pong. I need to keep control of where the ball is and where it is going next. This will insure that everyone in the group is involved in the process and keep any one person from dominating the discussion. It is very important to continue this technique to insure that everyone who gives feedback feels as though you listened and understood their comments. After John gives his feedback I would say, "So I understand you correctly John, you feel that while business owners need their personal and business finances to work together, you feel the greatest challenge that they face is hiring and retaining good people. Did I understand you right?" After he confirms I will move on to the next person, "Sally, you heard both John and Bill, how do you feel about this issue?"

If you simply implement that strategy, you will have a very active and controlled discussion involving everyone in the room. The conversation will flow well and everyone will walk away feeling as though they contributed to your objectives and gave you the help that they had set out to give you. They will also feel as though their opinions were heard and valid. This is a critical component to these groups.

If you simply continue to use the Verbal Ping Pong method throughout the group, the discussion will flow from question to question. You will want to keep in mind the time constraints to insure that you move on to your follow up questions and get through the questions that you have for the group. The common mistake that many of the professionals that I work with make is that they get involved in the discussion and begin to run over on time. If this happens, the questionnaire will suffer and so will your results. It is important to stop the discussion to give adequate time for the questionnaire.

The Questionnaire

I always leave a minimum of ten minutes for the completion of the questionnaire. Even when the conversation is going very well with the group, I insure that I stop the group with ten minutes to go. I will say, "I appreciate the discussion that we are having and wish we could continue it. In the interest of sticking to the agenda, we need to move on to the questionnaire. I have allotted ten minutes to complete it so we should have plenty of time. I will leave the room to begin to prepare the food, please answer each question on there as thoroughly as you possibly can. That written feedback is going to be very valuable to us."

I always leave the room for them to complete the questionnaire. If you do, they will quietly put their heads down and thoroughly answer the questions. If you stay in the room, they will ask questions, keep talking, and you will not get the answers to the questions that you need. Always have a reason to leave the room and tell them you will come back into the room in ten minutes. I will typically have food for focus group participants and will need to leave the room to get the food prepared.

The Food

While it seems simple, the food is actually a very important part of the focus group structure. When you complete the focus group, everyone will immediately leave unless they have a reason to stay. Even if they have additional comments or questions you will rarely hear them because they will assume the group is over and it is time to leave. That is why I have food for the participants. I will always have something very simple like sandwiches or pizza at the very end of the group. I also have "to go" boxes available for the participants who need to get going. I am aware that I have asked for one hour of their time and I have used that. The "to go" boxes are available for them to grab some food and get going if they need to. For those who want to stick around and ask questions or give additional feedback, I tell them that they can certainly stick around and enjoy some food. This is the time that is great for interacting with clients, getting more feedback, having clients offer opportunities for your business in the form of referrals and introductions, and just simply continuing to build your relationships.

If you are using the Client Centered Focus Groups to introduce a new product or service and gain feedback, interested clients will stick around and want to talk more about the product or service. Some will want to schedule time to discuss it further. This will typically happen when the food is there. They will stay an additional half hour to an hour and converse together and with you. This is a sign that you have conducted an excellent discussion. When people want to stick around and talk rather than leave, they are showing you that they enjoyed the time.

At the conclusion of the group, you want to gather the questionnaires and sincerely thank them for their participation. If they had questions or comments that require your follow up, insure them that you will contact them to follow up with a response. And then, relax, the hard part is over. Now you need to assess the groups' feedback, identify opportunities to improve and expand your business, and use the information available to you to continue to grow your business.

Step 8 – The Follow Up

I recently had lunch with a client as a follow up to his first sessions with his clients. It had been three months since his first set of Client Centered Focus Groups. When we had last spoken, he was overwhelmed by all of the things that he learned and all of the opportunity that had presented itself in the first focus group.

Among the feedback he received was specific input about his newsletter that he spent a lot of time and money on. Clients told him that the information was too confusing and recommended something that he thought was an "incredible" alternative. They recommended that instead of mailing a piece that isn't personalized and filling it with content that people don't understand, that he should do a monthly teleconference that any of his clients could call and join. He could give an overview of the content of the letter and then have a real discussion with his clients to discuss the markets, what was happening, and field questions. This entire process would take him an hour per month and his clients all agreed that they would really appreciate it.

On top of that, two of the participants recommended that he speak directly with certain relationships that they had about his service. Basically, they had come across referral opportunity recently and were not thinking of him when they did. Now that they were in front of him in the focus group, he was top of mind and they recommended that he speak with them as they had problems he could solve. Finally, one of his clients recommended that he address a large group that the client was part of and educate them about topics in his subject area.

Three months later as we sat at lunch and I asked the client how things had progressed he looked at me as though he was defeated. He admitted that "things were crazy" and that he had not taken the clients advice on the monthly teleconference idea, although he intended to "soon." He had not contacted the clients who had people that he needed to meet and had not schedule a speaking appearance to the large group. The focus group is not the success of this process, the follow up is.

This requires making changes to your business based on feedback and following up on opportunity. You wouldn't be reading this material if you were not interested in making some changes in your business. Whether it is increasing the value your clients receive or building your business through becoming more referable, you have to follow up in a structured way.

I always use the information that I get from Client Centered Focus Groups in the exact same way as I use the information from Interactive Client Surveys. As I said from the onset, these two processes are almost interchangeable in development and implementation. I recommend that you follow the exact same steps for follow up that are recommended in the previous section. Rather than ask you to flip back and forth, I will reprint the follow up section on how to use the information.

Client Follow Up

One of the great things about conducting Client Centered Focus Groups consistently is that the follow up to the meetings is effective and extremely manageable. Unlike many group activities you only need to block about a half hour to take the action steps necessary to insure that your client knows that their time was well spent, and that it was appreciated. Now you need to take the next steps toward following up on the opportunity that they offered.

I always recommend that you should block the half hour just after the discussion to organize notes, your thoughts, and review the questionnaire that the clients left behind. I always try to analyze three specific areas between the discussion and the questionnaire:

- Did I learn more about how my client perceives my value?
- Did I learn how to improve the experience that my clients have so that I can increase my ability to be referred?
- Did I identify any resources that they have available to them to introduce me to the right kind of people?

If you noticed in the examples provided in this section, I focused equally on these three points. I want to insure that I have a clear understanding of how they view my value, how to improve their experience, and how to approach them about expanding my business. These three categories are the main measuring stick that I recommend. If you say "no" to any of the three, you need to revisit the discussion questions and questionnaire questions to insure that you are asking questions that cover that area. You have got to have a balance of all three.

During the half hour after the focus group, I will break my notes into these three categories so that I can begin to design my follow up. At the end of a meeting, my notes may say something like:

**note-I recommend breaking down these notes for each participant in a focus group.

WHAT IS MY VALUE

Client felt like:

- *I have worked to develop trust and have always been straightforward with them.*

- *I was a good listener and carefully consider alternatives before giving my advice.*

Client:

- *Sees my service as unique and very valuable to the needs of business owner.*

- *Did not understand that I provide investment and insurance services.*

WHAT CAN I IMPROVE

Client:

- *Felt like more one-to-one time may help alleviate some of their concerns.*

- *Thought that I sometimes confuse them with information and over assume their level of understanding.*

- *Mentioned that they have been considering some alternative products to what they have, and wanted to set a time to discuss those additional products.*

WHAT OPPORTUNITY MAY EXIST

Client:

- *Said that I need to be more consistent in communicating the business part of my practice and defining who I want to meet.*

- *Had a friend who owns a business that was looking for good resources to help them.*

- *Is chair of Business Owner Association and recommended that I speak at an upcoming event.*

These are the kind of comments that will be extremely common. I will use each of them in my approach to the client. First, I want to insure that I thank them for finding value in the services that I provide. Secondly, I want to insure that the advice to improve did not fall through the cracks and follow up on their needs, especially the fact that they want to learn about new products. Finally, I want to follow up on the friend that may need help and the speaking opportunity with my client. After writing these notes down, I wrap my half hour by identifying clear action steps and scheduling the time to complete the tasks. It should not take more than an additional half hour but is certainly worth it. I would much rather follow up with a current client on a friend that needs help and a speaking engagement than spend a half hour cold calling.

There are several methods of follow up after the Client Centered Focus Group. The key is not in how you follow up, it is that you do follow up and that there is a clear action that takes place. The main methods of follow up are by phone or in a letter. My preference is to do both. A letter shows that I took the time to sit down and write a very specific thank you letter to them, and a phone call allows me to schedule the next action.

An example of the letter I would send based on the notes above would be:

Dear John,

I want to thank you for participating in my Client Centered Focus Groups. I had asked you for the time because I have a high level of respect for you and knew that you would bring good advice with you. I want to let you know that the information you provided in the focus group was very helpful.

First, I want to let you know that I am glad to hear that your family feels that I am trustworthy and a good listener. These are skills that I have worked hard at and I am glad to see that it doesn't go unnoticed. I also am glad to hear that you feel my focus on business owners is the right move. Your feedback in that regard was really helpful.

I want to let you know that I will be calling you to schedule a time with you and Lisa to discuss the issues you brought up regarding meeting and discussing specific products. I agree that the market has changed and we should definitely be doing that for you.

Finally, thank you for your kind offer to recommend your friend who owns a business to me. As you know, I will certainly lend them an ear and give them any advice that I can. I will follow up with you on the same phone call to schedule an appointment regarding your friend, and speaking to the Business Owner Association. Your ideas and your resources are so helpful. The fact that you shared them with me is very much appreciated. I will look forward to calling you and meeting with you and Lisa again.

Respectfully,

Dan Allison

Obviously I will follow up that letter with the phone call I mentioned and follow through with my promise. If you think about this one example, I accomplished a lot with a simple focus group:

- I increased the satisfaction of a respected client by simply involving them.
- I sealed the retention of that client.
- I clarified my value statement and to whom I want to offer the services.
- I created a client who has a clear vision of who to recommend to me.
- I learned what my client finds valuable about my service.
- I identified areas of concern that can easily be addressed.
- I identified a need that may lead to additional service and revenue.
- I received an opportunity to meet a new client.
- I received an invitation to speak to 100 potential new clients.

These are not abnormal results. There is so much opportunity in your business model. There are so many connections and resources within your client base. Think of all of the executives, marketing experts, social networkers, business owners and managers that exist in your client base. The power of their knowledge and advice is limitless.

In Conclusion – Client Centered Focus Groups

Focus groups are not a new idea. They are used every day by large companies throughout the country as a means of understanding client loyalty and values. They are also a great way for companies to introduce new products and services to their customer base and gain honest feedback on the true value of the product or service.

As you have read, having a client base that truly understands your offering and what you want to accomplish is very powerful and productive. Having a client base talk to you about your business model, your value, and giving you recommendations is also a very powerful thing. The combination of the two is what Feedback Marketing is all about. Business is never a one way street. You can talk too much and listen too little and accomplish nothing. Conversely, you can talk too little and have a large group of loyal clients that are completely uninvolved in your business.

Client Centered Focus Groups will give you an unprecedented way to involve your best relationships in your business model in one of the most professional environments that you could possibly establish. It will benefit you, it will benefit them, and it will improve your business and grow your business. The greatest thing of all, it will cost you next to nothing. Listening is the cheapest marketing tactic you will ever use.

As you have seen, Interactive Client Surveys and Client Centered Focus Groups are very similar in structure and purpose. You can implement the two interchangeably or as a complement to one another.

If you have dedicated your career to serving a certain population and providing them with things that they value and are compelled to tell others about, these strategies will only help you in that effort.

I have never promoted focus groups as a clever way to sell stuff. I don't believe in that approach. I believe that through truly caring about what people value and listening to their feedback, they are sold on you and your product. Your products and services can be commoditized; your level of professionalism and the trust you develop cannot be.

I recommend that these strategies become more than a one-time experiment; focus groups should become an integral part of your business. By administering Interactive Client Surveys and Client Centered Focus Groups on an ongoing basis, you will have strategic information to make a dramatic impact on your career and the relationships that you have.

We have spent 43,000 words on serving your current clients and leveraging what you have to continue to build a solid business. There is however an entire population that we have not yet talked about. That population is a combination of all of the people that should be using your service but do not. What do they think of the services that you have for them? How do they feel about the value of your products and services? What are they looking for from a professional like you? What can you do to earn them as a client?

FM

PROSPECT CENTERED FOCUS GROUPS

Let Groups of Your Prospects Tell You How To Approach Them

YOU WILL GAIN

- An unprecedented way to get face time with qualified prospects in a non selling, comfortable environment
- An inexpensive and professional way to consistently present your products or services to quality prospects
- Valuable feedback on your products and services and what element is most appealing to your prospects
- Valuable feedback on your products and services and what elements to improve to be more attractive to prospects
- New clients and advocates through professional interaction with quality prospects
- A predictable format to gain feedback on your marketing concepts and ideas from the people that you market to

PROSPECT CENTERED FOCUS GROUPS

Hopefully you have read through the other two sections and did not just skip forward to this section to learn how to use focus groups to compliment your prospecting efforts. Many professionals focus all of their efforts on prospecting and fail to realize the opportunity that exists within their own client base. If you have skipped to this section and you currently have clients that are valuable to you, go back and implement Interactive Client Surveys, Client Centered Focus Groups, or both. There is no point in pouring water into a bucket that has holes in it. Fix the holes before you worry about finding more water. That said, let's explore how Prospect Centered Focus Groups can be one of the most powerful, inexpensive, profitable "marketing" efforts that you will use. I put marketing in quotes because most people don't realize that focus groups are in fact effective marketing tools in addition to being wonderful tools for improving business.

As I mentioned in the previous sections, many of us work hard to develop products, services, and other tools for a specific group of potential clients. We worked hard at developing solutions to their problems. We develop our solutions carefully and then work to develop marketing material that accurately communicates to the population how valuable the services or products are. Many times however, the target market does not respond the way that we want them to. They don't line up outside of our doors to experience our "value added" services that is clearly different from that of our competitors. What is wrong with these people? Don't they understand how incredible we are? Don't they understand that we can change their lives with our services and products? What don't they get?

These are questions that we have all asked ourselves time and time again. We become frustrated that people choose our competitors and not us. We are certain that they will respond to a mailing campaign only to find out that the phone doesn't ring. When we do get face time with them and present our services they respond with a polite, "We'll be in touch." This is a frustrating reality for anyone who is in business trying to attract new clients. One of my clients marketed their services through conducting frequent seminars and workshops for their target market. They spent thousands on direct mail advertising to tell individuals how to attend the workshops and receive information on something that they would, no doubt, find valuable. After ten years of conducting workshops with unsatisfactory results — they were frustrated.

Their first area of frustration was in trying to understand why more people were not responding to the message on their mailer. They had to mail thousands of people to get even 20-30 people to attend their workshop. Why weren't they responding to the mailer in greater numbers? Was the topic wrong? Did it seem too sales-driven and not educational enough? Did it fail to address the challenges that they actually had?

118

Their second area of frustration was with the 20-30 people who actually showed up to the workshop. They would participate in the workshop, eat a nice meal, thank the company for the great information, and then walk out the door. The workshop was designed to get them to want to engage the company's services but a small portion of them actually did. Was the content not compelling enough? Was it difficult for the participants to understand the information that was shared? Were the presenters perceived as salespeople instead of providing an effective service? How could they work to get a better return on the investment they were making?

These are common issues for anyone who markets their services. Marketing requires the company providing the products or services to really understand the unmet needs of their target clients. It requires the company to clearly articulate a solution that helps the target consumer with the problem. Finally, it requires the fee for the service to seem fair for the value the customer experiences. The problem with being a business professional is that we sometimes think that we understand all of these things better than we do.

Do we truly understand the greatest challenges of the target market we are trying to serve? When the potential client hears a presentation or sees a marketing piece communicating how our service will solve a problem, do they really believe that it will? What are the objections that our customers have to using our services? Does our price align with our value?

All of these questions can be answered by using one very simple technique: Prospect Centered Focus Groups. At their foundation, focus groups represent a group of similarly situated people who come together in a room to hear a presentation about a topic or product that is geared toward solving problems that they have. After hearing the presentation, they give feedback on what they liked about it, what they didn't, and what would make people like them become users of the product or service. The fact that many can become users of the products or services after understanding them and seeing them explained is a secondary, but largely ignored benefit.

In the case of my clients who conducted the workshops, they simply wanted to understand how to get more people to show up to their workshops and how to make more of those who did show up, later become clients. The answer to all of their questions was lying right in front of them. The only people who could answer their questions were the people who had received the mailer and not responded and those who had been to the workshop and not taken the next step.

We developed small focus groups to find the answers to their challenges. We called former workshop attendees and offered them a small gift card in exchange for their time and opinions to come in and answer some of our questions. We quickly filled up several focus groups with 8-10 participants. Imagine my clients surprise when many of them explained that they came to learn about the topic but found the presentation rather confusing. The topics were covered too quickly and there were too many of them. The numbers in the presentation didn't help the company prove their point, it confused their audience.

After several of these focus groups, the company was able to take their recommendations and improve the workshop which improved their conversion ratio. One simple process improved their marketing which through the coming years will make them hundreds of thousands of dollars more than they were. All this was possible through listening to the people they were marketing to. In addition to all of the great feedback, many of the people in the groups identified their own challenges that they came to the workshop to gain information on. The company was able to provide the information they had failed to the first time and gained new clients. This is a good illustration of the power of Feedback Marketing and Prospect Centered Focus Groups.

Sometimes, our boards of directors, highly compensated business consultants, and corporate executives don't have the answers to the challenges that we face; our customers do. Sometimes the answer can't come from those who already use our service; it has to come from those people that we wish were using it. When will it ever go out of style to stay on top of what our prospects challenges are and what they find valuable or appealing about our services?

Prospect Centered Focus Groups are a perfect complement to any business professionals marketing plan. It provides an opportunity to find out why a service doesn't work after we have tried it, and it allows us to see if something will work before we try it. My client who does workshops will never again spend thousands of dollars marketing a workshop without piloting it first through focus groups. The focus group is the ultimate marketing consultant.

This section will focus on how business professionals and organizations can use Prospect Centered Focus Groups to market and improve their organization. The latter is incredibly important. These focus groups have to be designed to learn what people value and how to approach them. Focus groups for prospective clients cannot be used as a "clever" way to fill up rooms of prospects and market to them. This strategy will backfire.

Prospect Centered Focus Groups are an inexpensive, professional, and ethical way to accomplish many objectives for a professional organization that has a mission to be the best in the field and provide services and products that their prospects respond to and value.

This section is a step by step process for designing and implementing Prospect Centered Focus Groups. While the steps involved in the process mirror the steps involved in conducting focus groups with current clients, the approach needs to be a little different because there is little trust developed at this point. The details are very important when implementing these focus groups. When implemented effectively, these focus groups will allow you to:

- Gain predictable face time with pre qualified prospective clients.
- Present any concept, product, or service that you want to be valuable to those prospective clients.
- Identify the most pressing unresolved challenges that prospects have.
- Learn whether or not the products or services connect with the population and solve the challenges you are working to solve.
- Learn what objections your prospective clients have to the service that you provide so that you can adjust your offering accordingly.
- Familiarize prospects with your products and services so that they can advocate for them.
- Gain new clients through the exposure that focus groups provide.

While these focus groups can be very powerful, they should not be overused. You will find in your business that if you simply implement Interactive Client Surveys with your current clients one hour per week, conduct a Client Centered Focus Group four times per year, and Prospect Centered Focus Groups four times a year, you will have a bullet-proof marketing plan and business model and will be introduced to more opportunities than you can manage.

Think about that example above; what would happen to your business if you did one Interactive Client Survey a week, one Client Centered Focus Group a quarter, and one Prospect Centered Focus Group a quarter? You would have met one-to-one with 50 clients, involved 40 more in focus groups, and met 40 new prospects through focus groups. Do you think that may lead to a better business and more opportunity for growth? Feedback Marketing is best used as a combination of all three strategies. If you focus too much on prospects you will lose a client for every prospect that you turn into a client. It is akin to running on a treadmill — it may produce activity but you will not be anywhere further than when you started.

Step 1 – Identifying What Your Challenges Are

The first step toward implementing Prospect Centered Focus Groups is to clearly outline what challenges you are facing in your business model that your prospects may be able to help you with. Most of the time, these are challenges with how you market the services that you provide. Whether you are trying to figure out how to market your products or services most effectively or are trying to figure out why an existing product or service is not being received as well as you would like it to, prospective clients are very helpful in pointing you in the right direction.

As is true with each of the three strategies in the Feedback Marketing System, I recommend that you follow each step. Even if you feel as though you already know what your challenges are, I recommend that you write them down so that you are able to clearly articulate to anyone what the challenges are. This is a helpful exercise for defining your purpose and your clear objectives. For this section, I will use a large banking client for my examples.

This banking client had a good market presence and a well-established brand in their community. They had dozens of branches and a great client base. As many banks do, they continued to assess what services could be added to their offering to capture more of their banking clients business and serve them in more ways. Anyone in business would agree that the more reasons your client uses your service, the better your retention of those clients will be.

The bank had assessed what unique opportunities existed in their market place and decided that they would complement their mortgage and finance division through adding real estate services. The bank became a real estate brokerage firm with the intention of helping banking clients buy and sell real estate. A natural by-product of being involved in the real estate activity would be increased mortgage activity. Because they had the resources that no other real estate firm had, they would also provide their real estate selling services for less money than the competition. While the real estate division would be a profit center, the real money was in securing the financing for the real estate.

The bank decided to use its brand in the marketing and the price as it was truly the unique selling proposition. The bank was spending an average of $25,000 per month in print media to educate their customers and the public that they sold homes for less than the competition did. Although they spent a lot of money to make the phone ring, the calls that came in did not match the investment in marketing. They listed their challenges as:

The public is not responding to the print media marketing that we are doing.

We do not know if people do not see the ads or if they do see the ads and don't respond.

If they see the ads and don't respond, we need to understand why consumers would not respond to something that could so obviously save them thousands of dollars.

We don't know if consumers are confused by the bank providing the real estate services or if they simply don't trust that a bank would be as good as a real estate firm.

We need to identify whether the bank helps the branding of the service or if our customers feel the brand hurts the service.

These are common challenges any time that an organization adds services that may be outside of its core offering. We all feel as though we are adding the things to our offering that our consumers want, but, do we really involve the consumers in that process? Take the time to thoroughly list what challenges you are facing with marketing your services and getting your customers to respond to your service. Do you want to get more people through your doors with your marketing? Do you want the people who come through your doors to be more excited by your service or products? Are your current customers prospects for a different service? Write down the challenges that you face and then move on to Step 2 to identify why you want to do focus groups.

Step 2 – Developing Your Purpose Statement and Objectives

Your purpose and objectives are critical to every step of this process. Before moving on to develop your focus groups you need to have a firm grasp on your challenges and what your objectives are. Typically, your objectives are the opposite of your challenges. In essence, you want to overcome the challenges through using focus groups. As with your challenges, I recommend that you take the time to explain your purpose and objectives in a written format. Your purpose and objectives will be critical in many areas of your future development. You will need to be able to clearly articulate your challenges and objectives to your prospects in many key areas of implementing this process. You will need to use them to:

- Invite participants on the phone and in person to attend the group.
- Develop the structure for your focus groups and in explaining to the group why you are doing focus groups and what you want to accomplish.
- Develop the questions that you will ask the focus group to discuss.
- Develop the written questionnaire that you will ask participants to complete.

- Assess the effectiveness of the focus group and develop a
  follow up plan.

Your purpose and your objectives are similar to having a business plan with clear cut goals. If you don't have one, you have no blueprint to work from and no measuring stick for success. While your purpose may evolve as you develop the focus group, it is important to have them written for frequent review. For the banking client that I worked with, their purpose for conducting focus groups and their objectives were as follows:

- *Through conducting focus groups, we want to increase our prospects understanding and use of the service that we have developed. We want to make our marketing efforts more effective and want to brand the service in a way that does not create confusion in our market place. Specifically, we want to:*

1. *Gather several groups of 8-10 home sellers to participate in the focus groups.*
2. *Learn what kind of read rate our print media advertising is getting.*
3. *Gain feedback on our target markets perception of the service through having seen the print media advertising.*
4. *Fully communicate to the home sellers how the home selling process works and why it is less expensive than the competition.*
5. *Learn what impressions of the service home sellers have after they fully understand it.*
6. *Learn what objections our prospects have to using the service.*
7. *Learn what our prospects see as the most valuable component of the service.*

As you can see, the banks objectives are very straight forward and quite simple. They want to get a room full of their prospects and ask them if they have seen the advertising and what their impression is of the advertising. After that, they will clearly present how the home selling service works to the prospects and get their feedback on various aspects of the process. This is why

I call the process Feedback Marketing. You are able to market your services while you are learning from your prospects. Think about it, if the ads that the bank was placing resulted in an hour with ten qualified prospects to clearly present how the service works, the ad would be very effective. While they explore how to improve the ad, they are getting results that the marketing effort was trying to achieve.

This allows any business owner or organization to market their services and products while they are improving their services and products. It allows you to work on your business and in your business at the exact same time. Assuming that the bank compensated focus group participants $50 per household, they were able to educate and learn from nearly 500 prospective clients as focus group participants for the same amount of money they were spending on their print media marketing each month. It is the perfect balance of creating brand awareness and marketing in a comfortable environment. For those who want to use the service, that is great but you will also learn what they saw as valuable which will help in future marketing efforts. For those who would not use the service, you are able to learn what to improve to make the service more effective. You win in both scenarios and so does the focus group participant.

Most of the time, when you make a list of the objectives that you hope to accomplish in the focus group, you will need to educate them on what your products or services are to get the feedback you seek. You have to educate them about your company to receive feedback. Marketing is occurring while you are receiving feedback.

After writing down your list of challenges and the purpose and objectives of the focus group, you will need to clearly identify who you would like to approach to attend the focus groups. While this is not as easy as conducting Client Centered Focus Groups because the relationship is not there; most organizations and professionals have many different areas to pull from to fill up their focus groups.

Step 3 – Identifying Participants

One of the most important components of any focus group is insuring that the people in the room giving you feedback on your products and services are qualified to give the feedback. That is to say that you need to insure that you qualify anyone that you allow in to the focus group. This is actually quite beneficial on many levels. Any process that allows you to qualify people before you spend any time on them makes sense. Most of the time, we don't have the credibility to qualify people prior to meeting them. In this case, it is different. In a focus group, you have to qualify the people to insure that they do in fact meet your target market criterion and they are the people to which you market your products and services.

If you are marketing a new service to business owners, people who do not own businesses are not going to give you the right kind of feedback on the service. If you are marketing to a specific kind of business (i.e., $1 million to $5 million in revenues), then you will have to qualify that list even further. Whatever your parameters, you have to insure that you have the right people in the room.

This may be difficult to do prior to actually talking to them on the phone or in person because we don't often have a lot of detailed information on the people that we want to approach. There are many different places to look for people to participate in your focus groups.

Current Clients Who Are Prospects for a Different Service

Sometimes, your current clients are also prospects. Meaning, we often acquire somebody as a client using one of our services but they don't use other products or services that are available to them. In this case, these people are ideal for Prospect Centered Focus Groups. There is some built in trust because they use you for a different service and you know more about them than you would somebody off the street. If there is a potential for your current clients to use more of the services that you offer, they are great participants for focus groups.

Former Respondents to Your Marketing Efforts

The information held in your database may be a gold mine for future Prospect Centered Focus Groups. Often, we meet people throughout the course of doing business and for one reason or another they don't become clients of our service. You may put these people in your database and continue to mail to them or market to them; but, whatever you are currently doing is not working. How do I know? If your marketing was connecting with them they would be clients by now. Wouldn't it be helpful to learn what challenges they have, what they value, what products or services they may be interested in and what they would respond to? People inside of your database are the perfect candidates for Prospect Centered Focus Groups.

Clients of Professional Relationships

Most organizations and businesses have professional relationships with other people who have influence over the kind of people they want to do business with. We often call these referral relationships. If you have relationships with influential companies or people, they are a great referral source for focus groups. Rather than calling these people to ask, "Do you know individuals who can use my service?" you can contact them to explain your purpose and objectives for conducting focus groups and ask if they know anyone opinionated enough to participate. This has been very successful for many of my clients. These relationships most of the time would be happy to help us in our efforts; this gives them a very easy way to do so.

Current Client Referrals

Much like the clients of our professional relationships, your current clients also may be a quality source of referrals for Prospect Centered Focus Groups. People will typically socialize with other people like them. Therefore, they are often able to recommend people who have similar traits for focus groups. If you call your clients who fit the profile of the people you are trying to conduct focus groups with and ask if they know anyone who may be a good fit, you may fill up several groups. Again, you will begin to understand how important it was to document your challenges and objectives. You have to explain this to your clients or professional relationships in a way that makes sense to them. When they understand the challenges that you face and what you are trying to accomplish, many will be happy to help.

Former Workshop or Seminar Participants

Many organizations spend thousands on public workshops or seminars and have a very small percentage of those who participate become clients. Wouldn't it be helpful to know what the people who attended were looking for so that you know what you didn't deliver? Remember, you are able to qualify them so they will not be tire kickers. They will be people who are a fit for the services or products that you attempted to promote through the use of workshops and seminars.

These people are often excellent candidates for Prospect Centered Focus Groups because you already know that they are the kind of people who will leave the house in search of something. That is why they came to the workshop or seminar in the first place. Going back to these people is among one of the most beneficial things that you can do. Chances are you spent quite a bit of money to get in front of them only to have them slip through your fingers. Go back to them and ask them what you could have provided to get a different result.

Purchased Lists

While ninety percent of my clients are able to fill up several focus groups using the resources already mentioned, some are at the point in their career that they need to buy a list. While this is the least effective of the methods mentioned, it will still be effective. The challenge with buying the lists is that you are never really sure how good the information is from the list. If you find a company that provides quality information, stick with them because there are not very many. You will want to insure that you gather a phone number. Direct mail is not as effective as placing phone calls, however; many of my clients do direct mail.

These methods should be very effective to get a quality list of potential Prospect Centered Focus Group participants. You will find that the most difficult part of the invitation process is actually getting a hold of people on the phone. Beyond that, most people are very receptive to the phone call. Once you do a few focus groups, you will realize that it will actually become easier to fill them up. You will realize how frequently you are already in front of the right kind of people but really haven't maximized the opportunity. Inviting those people to focus groups is a great way for you to use their experience to build your business while educating them about your products or services. Once you have a list of prospects that you feel may be qualified to give you feedback and use your service, you will need to begin to put structure to the group before you begin inviting them to participate.

Step 4 – Structuring the Focus Group

On the surface, many focus groups would seem to be very open ended discussions with very little structure. In reality, most focus groups are highly structured with very clear agendas and objectives. Regardless of what profession you are in or what your objectives are, your focus groups will more than likely have four components to them and last roughly one hour.

It is important to have this structure clearly outlined and written out prior to starting the invitation process. It is very important that you understand how the focus group will flow, what material will be presented, and what questions will be asked prior to filling up the room. Some people put the cart before the horse and find themselves at the eleventh hour trying to piece together the structure of the focus group. If you fail to plan with focus groups, you can plan to fail with focus groups. The first component of the focus group will be how you introduce the focus group to the participants. The Introduction is one of the most critical aspects of the group.

Introduction

It is first important to remember that we will cover all of the details about filling up the room, conducting the group, following up after the group and all of the other "how to" details. Right now, it is important to stay focused on structure. The first detail that you will want to write down will be how you plan to begin your focus group. The Introduction is probably the most important component of the focus group for several reasons.

The Introduction is the first 4 to 5 minutes of the group where you will outline why you decided to do focus groups, what your objectives are, and what will occur during the group. This should be a structured introduction so that you insure to cover all three of the areas I just mentioned. The Introduction serves the purpose of letting the groups understand what challenges led the company to conduct the focus group and what they are trying to overcome by doing so. It will also be the time to refer to the clear cut objectives that you want to accomplish by doing the focus group. If you recall, these are the objectives that you detailed in Step 2 of this process. Finally, you will let the group know what will occur over the hour of time that you have asked of them.

When participants arrive, they are always a little bit nervous. They are unsure what to expect, what they will have to do, and they will have forgotten why you have asked them to participate. It is very important to begin the focus group with a clear explanation of these things so that the participants can relax. When you explain the challenges that your firm has faced and why you are looking at prospects to help solve the problem, the idea is that it should make sense to the prospective clients. They have to understand the challenges and the objectives so that they understand what role they will play in accomplishing them.

Again, I recommend that you write your Introduction down to insure that you follow the structure I mentioned. The three key areas to cover in the Introduction are:

- Why did we decide to do focus groups?
- What are the objectives that we hope to accomplish by doing them?
- What will occur over the hour that we have asked of you?

If you recall, the bank was struggling to get the sellers of real estate to respond to the marketing efforts that they were employing. They wanted to explore what sellers thought of the services and understand how to market the service better. Below is an example of their full Introduction to the focus group:

I want to thank you all for agreeing to participate in this focus group. My name is Dan Allison, and I will be conducting the group on behalf of the bank. Before we begin, I want to give you a brief overview of why we decided to do some of these focus groups with home sellers, what we hope to accomplish by doing so, and what you can expect over the hour that we have asked of you.

Why Did We Decide to Do Focus Groups?

As some of you may know, our bank has experienced significant growth over the years. We have added branches throughout the community and continue to see our banking business grow steadily. As we have grown, we have continued to add services to try to meet the needs of our customer base and to attract new customers to the bank.

A couple of years ago, we decided to offer a home buying and selling service. Our rationale was simple in doing so. We believed that our customers and other people in the community were paying too much in real estate commissions when they sold their homes. We believed that we could use our presence as a bank to help people in the community sell their homes like a real estate brokerage without paying the high fees. We would be able to do so because we also finance real estate and don't need to make as much money on the real estate efforts.

While the business model seemed to make sense, we are not getting the traction that we thought we would in the marketplace. Despite spending thousands and thousands of dollars on marketing the service, people don't seem to be responding. We decided to conduct a series of focus groups with home sellers in this marketplace to better understand their needs, what their opinions are of the services that we developed, and understand how to market the services to home sellers better than we are now.

What are the Objectives that we Hope to Accomplish?

We have some very straightforward objectives that we hope to accomplish by conducting these focus groups. You will see the objectives listed on the one page agenda (discussed later) in your folders. I will review those objectives with you. The objectives that we would like your help in accomplishing are:

1. Learn what kind of read rate our print media advertising is getting.

2. Gain feedback on our target markets perception of the service through having seen the print media advertising.

3. Fully communicate to the home sellers how the home selling process works and why it is less expensive than the competition.

4. Learn what impressions of the service home sellers have after they fully understand it.

5. Learn what objections home sellers have to using the service.

6. Learn what home sellers see as the most valuable component of the service.

As you can see, we have very well-defined goals for the group, but we will only achieve them through getting honest opinions from people like the ones in this room.

What Will Happen During the Hour?

Over the course of the hour, we will have a very structured agenda. The first thing that we want to do is give you about a 20-minute overview of how the home selling process that we designed works. This will be what we would like the majority of the feedback on so if you would, pay special attention to anything in the presentation that you feel will help us accomplish the objectives I just explained. After giving you an overview of the service, we have designed four discussion questions. We would like your honest feedback. We will conduct the discussion for roughly 25 minutes. At that time, I will conclude the discussion and we will move on to the written questionnaire.

This questionnaire will be completed in roughly 10 minutes and will get us the remainder of the feedback that we are looking for. The food will come toward the end of the focus group to insure that we are not distracted during the discussion. Out of respect for your time, there are "to go" boxes should you need to box up the food and get going. For those of you who have additional comments or questions, feel free to stick around and grab something to eat; we will be happy to answer any questions and gain more feedback. We sincerely thank you for the time that you have given us. If there are no questions, we will begin the group with an overview of the home selling service that we designed and why we designed it the way that we did.

Notice the simple structure but how it clearly lays out what will happen over the time that the participants will be in the room? It is very straightforward. If you think about it, you are really saying, "We have been trying to get you to understand our service and we are not succeeding. We want everyone to sit and listen to what our service is and how it works and then we want to know why you would or would not use the service."

Pretty simple, but so frequently overlooked. If you simply communicate those three aspects in your Introduction, you will have a captive group of your targeted prospects ready to listen to you talk about your products or services and understanding that while you are presenting them to the group, you are really interested in their honest feedback. This will insure that the group is actively listening and taking notes to insure that they can play an active role in the discussion.

After developing the Introduction for the group, you will want to develop a "presentation" of sorts to communicate whatever it is that you want to get the feedback on. There are many different directions to go with the presentation portion of the group.

Presentation

In order for prospects to give you good feedback and advice on how to approach people like them with your products or services, they have to first understand what your products or services are. This is one of the great things about Prospect Centered Focus Groups. While you are able to get feedback from the kinds of people that you spend your days marketing to, you have to market to them to get the feedback.

Think about the bank that we have been talking about. They spend $25,000 per month trying to get home sellers to respond to their advertising with the end goal of having them come in so that they can understand the home selling service. The focus group allows the bank to accomplish that same objective in a much better environment, for less money, and they will learn a great deal about the people that they serve. It is a perfect balance of marketing and feedback. Too much marketing and not enough feedback will result in participants thinking they attended a seminar. Too much feedback without any marketing will result in prospects that leave the focus group uninformed about what you do and how you do it.

The presentations in focus groups are as varied as the professionals reading this book. Think about how many different professionals will read this book. All are focusing on different consumers and all have different products, services, and strategies designed to serve them. There are a few general topics for presentations in focus groups, but first, a couple of the details.

You want to keep the presentation portion of the focus group to no more than 20 minutes. You will find out very quickly that the discussions are what make these groups fun so don't eat into that time with a long presentation. The presentation can be in a power point format if you feel that would be most appropriate or each person can have a presentation piece to follow along. You may simply want to give them an outline of the key points that you want to hit in the presentation. The main presentation topics are:

A Unique Process

Like our bank, many companies have worked to develop a process to benefit their consumers. If you have a process that you have designed for a specific group of prospects, use your presentation time to give the prospects an overview of why you developed the process the way you did and what challenges it solves. You are more than likely conducting focus groups because you are trying to learn if they have the challenges you think they do and if the process actually does a good job of addressing them. This is an ideal topic for the presentation. Walk them through how the process works step by step. Think of them as a group who responded to an advertisement and came in to learn about the process you designed. How would you present to a group like that? The real benefit is that they will tell you if the process connects with them or if you have missed something that is important to them.

A Unique Strategy

Much like a unique process, unique strategies are designed to be appealing to a certain audience. The executive coaching firm in Section 2 had unique strategies for business owners to use to improve their business. The challenges they had were; 1) knowing whether or not they were indeed unique in the eyes of the business owners, and 2) if the strategies really did connect with the business owners. If you are a problem solver for a living you probably have strategies that your target market of prospects do not know exist and are impossible to market. Focus groups are a great place to explain what challenges the strategies solve and how they benefit the target consumer. Again, the real benefit is that you will learn if that is indeed the case.

A Unique Product

Many companies and professionals work with unique products that solve a challenge for their target consumer. While you may not have designed the product, it is still important to get feedback from prospects on how you explain the product and its value. This will not only be effective at getting the product in front of your target consumer, but also let you know what the key selling points are of the product and what objections your prospects have to using a product like the one you want to promote. These are very popular focus groups in the financial markets. Often, financial products are misunderstood by the consumers. Focus groups are a good way to get in front of the right prospects to present the products and then have a discussion about the prospects perceptions of the product.

A Unique Service

You will notice that many of the topics involved in focus groups have to do with having something unique. This is typical because the more unique a product or service is, the more difficult it is to educate the target market about it. If it doesn't fit into a box or if your prospects don't understand it, the marketing of it is very difficult. This is especially true when you have a unique service that addresses a consumer need. If it is unique, they probably have never experienced it and don't even know it is available. Focus groups are a good way to make them aware of the service and how it works while learning how to market it better. The feedback is helpful for you, and the ability to market it to prospects in person is priceless.

There are endless examples of what you can use to present in the 20 minutes that you have in your focus group. The key is that you need to insure that the presentation is what you plan to focus your discussion on. You can't use the presentation to pitch something and then not use the discussion time to ask questions about it. If you talk about a unique product, ask questions about how aware the prospects were of the product. Ask them what they see as the primary value of the product and what objection they would have to using the product. The same is true with unique services, processes or strategies. To give you feedback on what you have that is unique, they have to understand what you have in the first place. The presentation is the time to clearly explain to your prospects what your marketing has failed to do.

The Discussion

After introducing the purpose of the focus group to the participants and presenting the process, product, strategy or service that you want feedback on, you will want to move on to the interactive part of the focus group. For most people, participants included, the discussion is the most enjoyable part of the focus group. It is very interactive and informative. While we will get to "how to" conduct the discussion in a later section, here we need to focus on structuring the discussion.

As you have seen, you will use about 5 minutes to give the introduction, you will present your topic for roughly 20 minutes, and you will now want to conduct a discussion for roughly 25 minutes. While many people fear that they cannot keep people talking for 25 minutes, you will be very surprised. Almost all of my clients report running over on time because of the discussion portion of the focus group. We will talk later about how to keep the discussion going, but for now we need to focus on the actual questions.

For a quality discussion, you will want to prepare roughly four to five open ended questions to ask the group. We have discussed how to write open ended questions in other sections so I will just remind you that these are questions that don't elicit a one word response. They should require thought and require several sentences to answer. I always structure my presentations the same way so my discussion questions are always easy to write. My presentations always cover the following:

- The challenges that I perceive the prospects to have and why I developed the product, service, strategy, or process.
- How the product, service, strategy, or process works step by step.
- What the benefits are to the client who uses the product, service, strategy, or process.

Because I follow this method regardless of what I am presenting, my discussion questions follow a similar format. The questions that I want to focus on are:

- What do the prospects feel their greatest challenge is?
- What do they feel about the product, service, strategy or process that was designed to solve those challenges? Why is it valuable? Why isn't it valuable?
- What do they see as the most attractive benefit to using the product, service, strategy or process?

By asking questions that cover these three areas, you will learn how well you understand the struggles of your prospects while learning what issues each individual faces. You will learn what part of your presentation really connected with people and what they perceived to be the main value of what you presented. Finally, you will learn their perceptions of what benefit they would experience by using it. They will tell you why they would use it, and why they would not. Both of these things are critical to learn.

Our bank was presenting their real estate process for home sellers. If you recall, they thought that sellers were irritated by paying too much commission for too little service. They felt that this was the greatest challenge that their prospects faced. They were presenting their home selling process and how it is designed to solve those challenges. Finally, they were wrapping up the presentation by outlining the benefits that home sellers experience by using the service. The discussion questions that they designed to get the feedback that they were looking for were:

1. What do you see as the biggest challenge facing the home seller in today's market?
2. After hearing an overview of the service that we designed, what do you see as the most valuable component of the service and what it helps sellers accomplish?
3. What do you see as the primary drawback of using a service like the one that we described?
4. How would you recommend that we alter our marketing to be more effective at attracting home sellers?

These discussion questions proved to be very informative. While they learned a lot about their target market and how to market to them, many of the home sellers who participated in the focus group later used the service. The discussion questions should be designed to find out if you understand your consumers and what they think of your offering when they understand it. After developing the discussion questions that will consume the discussion period, you can address the other questions that you have on the questionnaire.

The Questionnaire

After developing your discussion questions, you will want to move on to developing additional questions for a questionnaire. The questionnaire is typically completed during the last ten minutes of the focus group. Unlike the discussion, these questions can also be rating style questions. I definitely recommend that you put many open ended questions on the questionnaire as well, but rating scale questions are a great compliment.

Rating scale questions are typically designed to assess how strongly someone feels about something. Open ended questions will tell you why they feel the way they do. An example of an open ended question would be:

• What do you see as the primary value of the product or service that was presented?

A rating scale question may ask:

• On a scale of 1 to 10, how well do you feel that this product or service addresses the needs that our customers have?

1 2 3 4 5 6 7 8 9 10
Not Well   Fairly Well   Extremely Well

As you can see, the rating scale will tell you how valuable the client thinks the product or service is, but the open ended question will tell you what about the product or service is valuable. They are both very important aspects to promoting a product or a service.

I recommend that you give participants one to two minutes per open ended question. If you plan to give them ten minutes to complete a questionnaire, you will need to insure that you don't place more than five open-ended questions on the questionnaire. Rating scale questions are much easier to complete and they will be able to answer several per minute. They are designed to get an immediate reaction rather than open ended questions which require a little more thought.

I typically develop about ten questions per questionnaire. Don't get fixated on the number of questions that you have on the questionnaire. Never compromise quality for quantity. Of the ten questions I typically develop, five are open ended and about five will be rating scale questions. On the following page, I have given a complete sample of the questionnaire used by the bank for their real estate services.

Name _____

Date of Focus Group _____

We want to thank you for your participation in our focus group. You have been asked to participate because we value and respect your input and feedback. This questionnaire is designed to gain additional feedback on questions that are vital to our growth and providing the level of service that we desire to provide to our current and future clients. We sincerely appreciate your thorough and honest answers to these questions. The answers will be used to help us provide an exceptional experience to our valued clients.

1. What was your understanding of the real estate services provided by ABC bank prior to this focus group?

2. How has your perception of the real estate services provided by ABC bank changed having been given an overview of the service if at all?

3. What do you see as the primary benefit that a home seller would experience through using the service that the bank provides?

4. What do you see as the primary drawback a home seller would experience through using the service that the bank provides?

5. On a scale of 1 to 10, how likely would you be to use a service like the one explained when you sell your home?

   1 2 3 4 5 6 7 8 9 1 0
   Not at all likely   Somewhat likely   Extremely likely

6. If you could change the way that we market this service to home sellers, what would you do?

7. On a scale of 1 to 10, how likely would you be to tell a fellow home seller about the service that you heard about?

   1 2 3 4 5 6 7 8 9 1 0
   Not at all likely   Somewhat likely   Extremely likely

Questionnaires are very effective to gain the insight of the consumers that you are trying to target. In the case of the bank, they were able to learn from their consumers that their $25,000 marketing campaign was confusing home sellers. They learned that most home sellers associated the banks "for sale" signs with foreclosed homes and thus did not see themselves as potential users of the service. They provided feedback on how the bank could more appropriately market the services so that people like them would understand them better. To put the icing on the cake, now that they understood the services, many inquired about how to use it to sell their home. The bank got to clearly market their service and the consumers gave valuable feedback and were respected for their time and opinions.

This is a perfect example of how Feedback Marketing works. After developing your questionnaire, you should have all of the structure put together for your focus group. You should know who you are approaching and what challenges you hope to solve. You should know how you will explain your purpose and objectives to the group and what presentation you want to give. Finally, you should know what questions you want to ask the group to discuss and give written responses to. Now it is time to fill up the room with the right prospective clients to give you the feedback that you are looking for.

Step 5 – Filling Up the Room

Filling up the room for Prospect Centered Focus Groups is much different than filling them up for Client Centered Focus Groups. With clients and relationships, there is an element of trust and a desire to specifically help you. With prospective clients, that element may not be there. You must therefore take a little different approach in the way that you explain the invitation to the potential participant, and the way that you respect them for their time.

The first difference is that you will more than likely need to provide some form of compensation for their time. This is to show them that their time and opinions are respected. In some industries, there is an issue with compensation because of compliance. I have worked in many of these industries and most compliance divisions are fine with the compensation as long as it comes in the form of a gift card and that it is clear to the participant that it is not inducement to do business or a rebate on past business. Without boring you to death with compliance language, I will leave it at that.

If you don't have compliance issues, I recommend cash rather than some form of gift card. Everyone likes cash and it can be used for anything. Think about receiving a gift, would you rather have a $50 gift certificate to a store or restaurant or would you rather just have the cash? That is why I recommend you provide cash if possible. If not, try to do a gift card that is the same as cash. This would be a Visa gift card or something that can be used anywhere. If that is not going to work for you, provide a gas card or a gift that everyone uses frequently. I recommend that you use $50 as your minimum compensation for a focus group. If you can get by with less, by all means do it. I just feel that $50 is a respectable amount and have always used that when conducting Prospect Centered Focus Groups.

With the issue of compensation cleared up, the next step is in the actual scripting for the phone call. You can use direct mail if you feel this is a better fit for your business but I can tell you from experience you do not get the response that you would by simply placing a phone call to the person that you want to participate. I don't feel like I was specifically selected from a group when I receive a bulk mailer. When I receive a personalized phone call, I feel much more respected. The Do Not Call List may apply. You will however find that there are thousands and thousands of people who are not on that list. You will also find that you don't need to call 100 people to get 1 participant. You should be able to fill up a focus group by contacting 30-40 people. If you are not getting that kind of ratio, you should check the list you are calling. Chances are they are not the right target market.

When you call them, they don't know you like they would if they were your client. It is important that they don't view you as some telemarketer who has been sent a list to call. They need to know that you are a higher level staff and that you are local. I also encourage you to say that you are inviting them to participate in a paid focus group right out of the gates. The goal of the initial piece of your invitation should be to get their attention and then simply ask them for permission to explain what you are inviting them to participate in. An example of the first piece of the invitation script for the bank would be:

Hello John, this is Dan Allison, I am the Vice President of ABC Bank here in Omaha. How are you? Great, I was calling to see if you would consider being a participant in a local paid focus group that our bank is conducting to get feedback from a select group of home sellers. Do you have a moment for me to explain what I am asking you to participate in?

It is very important that you mention a higher level title, the industry or company you are in, and that you are local. This stops people from thinking you are a telemarketer. Next, it is important to mention "local" again and "paid focus group" to the invitee. Finally, you should mention that you are asking a "select" group of whatever demographic they fall into. That could be seniors, business owners, female professionals, or whatever your target market is.

This paragraph is generally enough to peak their interest. It is rarely simply the compensation or they probably are not a good fit for what you have. They are normally intrigued by the idea of a focus group and the industry should appeal to them as well. If they are your target market, they are probably the kind of people who take an interest in your industry. Finally, there is an element of ego involved in being selected and feeling as though their opinions are important.

After gaining their attention and asking for permission to explain, you need to give them a summary of why you decided to do focus groups and what you want to accomplish by doing so. Remember I said your purpose statement and the objectives were going to be important later? This is where they come into play. You have to explain why you are doing focus groups in a way that makes sense to the person on the other end of the line. They have to feel like they will be able to give feedback and learn something themselves in addition to the compensation you will be offering. For the bank, the second piece of their invitation script was:

Thanks, you may or may not know that our bank developed a real estate service designed to save home sellers money when they sell their homes. We have marketed the services *extensively, but haven't received the response that we are looking for. We wanted to conduct a few small focus groups with home sellers to get their feedback on how the program works and how we market it. We are going to use the feedback to better communicate the program in our marketing. I think you would also find some of the content interesting as a home seller yourself. You would be one of eight people in a focus group and we are compensating $50 for the hour we are asking. Would you consider being part of one of our groups?*

This scripting is straightforward and very honest. It tells the participant that they are going to learn about the banks service and give feedback on it. It also explains that as the banks target market, they will probably enjoy some of the content. It allows the participant to come into an environment and learn about a topic that they care about, give their opinions, and be compensated for their time in an environment that they will trust. It is the perfect combination for the consumer.

You want to have anywhere from 8-10 people per group so you will want to get about 12 people to confirm attendance as you will have some drop off. The most difficult challenge is getting people to answer their phones. Even if they recognize the name of the company that comes over their caller ID they are not likely to answer. I always called from a local cell phone to increase the number of answers. This was helpful for me in insuring that I got to talk to people.

Unlike the Client Centered Focus Groups, you can delegate this phone call to one of your staff. You will need to insure that the staff member is talented on the phone. They must be the kind of individual who can talk to people without reading from a script. The more scripted this sounds the less effective it is. Remember, people want to feel like they were selected and having a drone read in a monotone voice from script doesn't accomplish that. If you have your staff do the calls, insure that they have buy in to why you are doing the groups and what you want to accomplish so that they can explain it to the invitee in their own way.

Again, the most important piece of the invitation script is that people need to understand why you are doing the groups and what your objective is so that it makes sense to them. If you can accomplish this with delegating the phone call, by all means delegate that phone call.

I typically recommend that you begin the invitation process about two weeks prior to the event. You will want it close enough to the event that the person considers their schedule but not so close that they already have commitments. I have had good success beginning my calls between 10 and 14 days from the group.

I try not to leave messages if at all possible. Unless there is a definite need to call back, most people don't. I switch up the times that I call people if they don't answer. If I try at 10 a.m. and don't get an answer, I will try at 3 p.m. I try to never call over the dinner hours as I hate it when people do that to me.

If you follow these rules and use a list that has quality prospective clients on it, you should have no problem filling up several focus groups. Once you get the person to confirm, you may want to mail a letter to them as a confirmation with the details of the group and the location to insure that they know where the group will be help. On the next page, I have given you an example letter to send out but I also recommend that you place a call 24 to 48 hours prior to the group with the following script:

Hello Bill, this is Dan Allison with ABC Bank. I was calling to confirm that I have you down for one of the eight spots for our upcoming focus group on Friday, July 9th. If for any reason you are unable to honor that commitment, please give us a call back so that we can fill the spot from our back up list. We will look forward to seeing you at 5:30 p.m. on that date. If you have any questions prior to the group, please contact me at 402-350-2532.

Dear John,

I want to sincerely thank you for agreeing to participate in our upcoming focus group. As we discussed on the phone, we are looking to receive feedback on the services that we designed for home sellers and the way that we currently market it. We have some very specific questions that will help us get the feedback from participants and are certainly glad that you have agreed to share your thoughts with our group.

As a reminder, the focus group will be held on October 25, 2010 from 11:30a-12:30p. We ask that everyone arrive a few minutes early out of respect for the limitations on time. We will hold the focus group at The Ivey which is located at XXXXXXXXXXX. We will serve food and refreshments to the group.

We have only reserved eight spots for this focus group so if something should come up, please let us know at your earliest convenience so that we may recruit from our back up list. Again, thanks so much for agreeing to participate. I will look forward to seeing you and receiving the feedback you will offer the group.

Respectfully,

Dan Allison
ABC Bank
Vice President

After filling up the room, you will need to insure that the stage is set and the environment is right. Setting the stage for the focus group and conducting the session is identical for both Client Centered Focus Groups and Prospect Centered Focus Groups. Rather than have you refer back to these stages in the previous section, I have re-written them using the bank as an example.

Step 6 – Setting the Stage

It is important to insure that from the moment people arrive until the moment they depart from your Prospect Centered Focus Group, you have structured an environment that is conducive to what you want to accomplish. This involves insuring that you have a professional environment that is free of distractions and all of your material in place prior to your attendees arriving.

The Environment

You want to insure that you secure a private location that is preferably in an office setting. If your offices have a conference room that is suitable for 10-12 people, it is an ideal place for the focus group to be held. The more you control the environment, the better you will be.

If your offices don't have an environment that is conducive to a private conference room setting for 10-12 people, you should think about the professional network that you have and who may have an environment that you can use. It is important that the environment say that you are there to work, not to entertain. These focus groups are about accomplishing objectives in a relatively small period of time. This means that you have to have very few distractions. If you don't have a professional network to work with, you may want to consider local libraries or universities. They often have rooms that are set up for this kind of environment.

One word of caution is to avoid restaurants at all cost. You will spend way too much time and money and at the end of the day will accomplish half of what you want to because of ordering, interruptions, and small talk that will occur naturally in this type of a social environment.

Within the private conference room that you have selected, you

148

will want to insure that you have a table that will comfortably seat 10-12 in a U shape or in a circle. You should never arrange the room classroom style. That style psychologically says that they are there to learn, and you are there to teach. The U shape or circle will show that you are there to interact and discuss.

If you can, you should select a room that has some windows as it can feel a bit tight in conference rooms that have no windows. This is not a necessity but it is nice. You will also want to insure that the temperature in the room is comfortable.

The Materials

You will want to prepare a folder with the materials for participants in advance so that everything is orderly. The first thing that you will want to place in the folder is an agenda. The agenda will look much like the agenda for an Interactive Client Survey. You should break it down into the key sections of the focus group. You should show the Introduction and list the objectives, the presentation of content, and the discussion and questionnaire time frames. An example agenda for the banking firm that we have been discussing is on the next page.

AGENDA FOR FOCUS GROUP
DATE

5:30-5:35 p.m.   INTRODUCTION AND OVERVIEW OF KEY
                   OBJECTIVES

-What lead us to conduct these groups?
-What will happen over the course of the hour?
-Covering our key objectives:

1. *Learn what kind of read rate our print media advertising is getting.*

2. *Gain feedback on our target markets perception of the service through having seen the print media advertising.*

3. *Fully communicate to the home sellers how the home selling process works and why it is less expensive than the competition.*

4. *Learn what impressions of the service home sellers have after they fully understand it.*

5. *Learn what objections our prospects have to using the service.*

6. *Learn what our prospects see as the most valuable component of the service.*

5:35-5:55 p.m.   PRESENTATION OF CONTENT

5:55-6:20 p.m.   FOCUS GROUP DISCUSSION

6:20-6:30 p.m.   WRITTEN QUESTIONNAIRE

6:30 p.m.   ADJOURN

Thank you for your participation

The agenda should be the first thing that participants see when they open the folder. The next thing that should be included in the folder is a copy of the presentation or content that you will be discussing with the group. If you are doing a power point presentation, you can print a copy of it with three slides per page. This will be used for participants to follow along with the presentation and take notes as you discuss the key points of the content. If you don't plan on giving a formal power point presentation but plan to give more of an overview of the business and the future objectives that you have for the business, you may want to simply do a one page outline. You want to insure that you stay on track to cover your key points. If you don't have a structure to follow, you will run the risk of talking too long or not covering everything that you want to cover.

Behind the copy of the presentation or the outline of your content, you want to place a copy of the questionnaire on your letterhead. While this will be completed later, I find it helpful for participants to review the questions as they wait for the group to start. This gives them an idea of what they will be giving feedback on and creates a more actively engaged group. When they know what they are expected to discuss, they will pay more attention to the content.

Also in the folder you will want a name tent for the participant to write their name and place in front of themselves. During the discussion, it is very helpful for them to be able to refer to each other by name and furthers the relationships and the intimacy of the environment. Name tags are difficult to read and often fall off so I recommend folding strong construction paper in half and using them as name tents.

The only other thing that you may want to give them in the folder would be a copy of an article that you feel may interest the group. This article serves no other purpose than to give them something to read while they wait for the group to start. Some people are not very comfortable socializing with people that they do not know. By placing the article in the folder, they will have something to focus on to insure that they remain comfortable.

At this point, you should have a good feel for why you are conducting the group and a very well thought out structure. You have your guest confirmed, the environment is ready and you have all of the materials organized in the folder. The only thing left to do is conduct the session.

Step 7- Conducting the Session

As with anything that you will ever do in business, focus groups will get easier the more that you do them. You will find your comfort zone and you will begin to have your own style. I can only give you the framework and the structure from my experience. You will need to make these groups your own based on your style. The key to making sure that you get everything that you want from the focus group and that your participants not only engage in but enjoy the group, is to know exactly what will happen from the time they walk in the door until the time that they leave. There are several key stages of conducting the group and it all starts with greeting the participants.

Greeting the Participants

I recommend that whoever will be conducting the focus groups actually meet the guests up front. I recommend that as you greet the guest and thank them for their "participation", you quickly review the contents of the folder you are giving them. I stress "participation" because that is what you want to continue to reinforce. You don't want to thank them for coming. You want to thank them for agreeing to participate.

If you just thank them and hand them the folder they will go into the room and sit down to begin going through the material in the folder. Because you have not walked them through what is in there they will probably initially wonder why there is a copy of a presentation. They may also begin to fill out the questionnaire even though you have not gone over the material necessary to complete it. Nervous people do strange things. It is important for you to go through the material so that they have a good understanding of what is in the folder. I always say the same thing. I recommend that you say:

Thanks for agreeing to participate in the focus group. Before you go into the room, I want to walk you through what is in this folder really quickly. Up front is a copy of the agenda for tonight, we only have an hour so we will insure we stay on track. Behind the agenda is a copy of the content that we will be sharing and asking the group for feedback on. Behind that is a questionnaire that we will complete at the end so if you would, hold off on completing that until then. Over on the other side is a name tent so that the participants can refer to each other by name. Finally, I put an article in there that I thought people might enjoy reading as we wait for the group to start. We are expecting 8 participants tonight and will begin just after 5:30 p.m.

Giving this brief explanation lets them know that while there is a presentation in there, it does have a point as it is what you want the feedback on. This is even more important with prospective clients as they don't have the trust in you that your clients will. It also insures that you don't have nervous people filling out questionnaires without any of the information that they will need to do so. Finally, it lets them know how many will be in the group which will make those first few people more comfortable. The first few people are always nervous that there will only be a few of them in the group.

Starting the Focus Group

I always begin just a couple of minutes behind because many people show up at the last minute for these groups. I normally will stop into the room very quickly to let the group know that we are waiting for a couple more people to arrive and will begin in just a few minutes. When the time arrives, you should go in and get seated at the head of the conference room table.

I always recommend that you stay seated the entire focus group. I feel like it is helpful for the group to feel like you are part of the group, not a presenter. When you stand up, you go into presentation mode and may begin doing some of the things that you don't even know that you do when you present to people. Remember, this is an environment that is supposed to be conducive to interaction. If you appear to be on stage that is less likely to happen.

As you sit down, begin with the five minute introduction that you have prepared. Our bank began with:

I want to thank you all for agreeing to participate in this focus group. My name is Dan Allison, and I will be conducting the group on behalf of the bank. Before we begin, I want to give you a brief overview of why we decided to do some of these focus groups with home sellers, what we hope to accomplish, and what you can expect over the next hour.

Why Did We Decide to Do Focus Groups?

As some of you may know, our bank has experienced significant growth over the years. We have added branches throughout the community and continue to see our banking business grow steadily. As we have grown, we have continued to add services to try to meet the needs of our customer base and to attract new customers to the bank.

A couple of years ago, we decided to offer a home buying and selling service. Our rationale was simple in doing so. We believed that our customers and other people in the community were paying too much in real estate commissions when they sold their homes. We believed that we could use our presence as a bank to help people in the community sell their homes like a real estate brokerage without paying the high fees. We would be able to do so because we also finance real estate and don't need to make as much money on the real estate efforts.

While the business model seemed to make sense, we are not getting the traction that we thought we would in the marketplace. Despite spending thousands and thousands of dollars on marketing the service, people don't seem to be responding. We decided to conduct a series of focus groups with home sellers in this marketplace to better understand their needs, what their opinions are of the services that we developed, and understand how to market the services to home sellers better than we are now.

What are the Objectives That We Hope to Accomplish?

We have some very straightforward objectives that we hope to accomplish by doing these focus groups. You will see the

*objectives listed on the one page agenda in your folders. I will
review those objectives with you. The objectives that we would
like your help in accomplishing are:*

1. *Learn what kind of read rate our print media advertising is
   getting.*

2. *Gain feedback on our target markets perception of the
   service through having seen the print media advertising.*

3. *Fully communicate to the home sellers how the home
   selling process works and why it is less expensive than the
   competition.*

4. *Learn what impressions of the service home sellers have
   after they fully understand it.*

5. *Learn what objections home sellers have to using the
   service.*

6. *Learn what home sellers see as the most valuable component
   of the service.*

*As you can see, we have very well-defined goals for the group,
but we will only achieve them through getting honest opinions
from people like the ones in this room.*

What Will Happen During the Hour?

*Over the course of the hour, we will have a very structured
agenda. The first thing that we want to do is give you about a
20 minute overview of how the home selling process that we
designed works. This will be what we would like the majority
of the feedback on so if you would, pay special attention
to anything in the presentation that you feel will help us
accomplish the objectives I just explained. After giving you
an overview of the service, we have designed four discussion
questions that we would like you to consider. We want your*

honest feedback. We will conduct the discussion for roughly 25 minutes. At that time, I will conclude the discussion and we will move on to the written questionnaire. This questionnaire will be completed in roughly ten minutes and will get us the remainder of the feedback that we are looking for.

The food will come toward the end of the focus group to insure that we are not distracted during the discussion. Out of respect for your time, there are "to go" boxes should you need to box up the food and get going. For those of you who have additional comments or questions, feel free to stick around and grab something to eat and we will be happy to answer any questions and gain more feedback. We sincerely thank you for the time that you have given us. If there are no questions, we will begin the group with an overview of the home selling service that we designed and why we designed it the way that we did.

After the introduction, you will move into your presentation of the content that you want to get feedback on. Again, the thing to keep in mind is that you should try to give an objective presentation. Try to stay away from using sales language when presenting your process, service, or products. Rather than say things like, "This is one of the great things that this will do for YOU," say, "This is one of the benefits that people experience from using this." Replacing the word YOU will make a big difference in the presentation.

Remember, you don't want to sell the people in the room. You want whatever you are presenting to be valuable to the larger demographic that these people represent. Focus your presentation of what the value is to the group of people as a whole, not the people specifically in the room.

As you present your topic, you should notice that people are taking notes and paying close attention to what you are saying. They are aware of what kinds of questions you will be asking the group to discuss after the presentation so they pay much more attention in a focus group than they may in a workshop or a seminar on the exact same topic. As you wrap up your presentation, you will want to transition into the group discussion. This is the point where these groups actually get to be a lot of fun. You can transition by saying something simple like:

That is the content that I wanted to share with a few of these groups. Now I want to move into the feedback portion of the group. As I told you at the beginning, I have prepared some questions that I would like to get the majority of the feedback on. The first question that I wanted to ask the group to discuss is: We explained our perception of the most common challenges that home sellers are facing, which challenges do you feel are accurate and what do you feel is the most pressing challenge facing home sellers?

The Discussion

Of all of the different pieces of conducting Prospect Centered Focus Groups, I believe the discussion causes the most anxiety for my consulting clients. They are normally fearful that nobody will talk or that there will be uncomfortable silence. They are nervous that one person will dominate the discussion or that people will become negative in the group. There is one technique that will eliminate all of these concerns and insure that your discussion involves everybody and flows very comfortably and smoothly. I call this technique Verbal Ping Pong.

After you ask you first discussion question, there will be a period of silence. Any time you have controlled the floor in front of a group and then turn the tables and ask them a question, there will be that period of silence. It seems like it lasts for thirty minutes even though it is normally only about five to ten seconds. I eliminate that period of time all together by using what I already know about people to begin the discussion. Before the group even starts, you should pick the person that you will call on to begin the discussion.

Pick the person that you can tell is a very social person and very comfortable in front of groups. These are always the people that seem full of energy and very happy and jovial. I always have their name written down in front of me when I begin the group so that I can avoid the awkward silence. So, to begin the discussion, I would ask the question and then immediately say, "And to avoid the awkward silence, Bill, would you mind starting off giving your feedback on that question?"

You will never run into a problem doing this. Normally, Bill will gladly lean forward and begin talking. Remember, these people came to a focus group. They knew that they would be the ones talking; they just need you to continue to conduct the session. While Bill is giving his feedback, you will obviously want to be actively listening to him. You may even want to jot down some notes if he says something that you want to remember. I always audio record the sessions as well and nobody ever seems to mind.

This insures that I can pay attention to the participants of the group. When Bill completes his thoughts, I will begin using the Verbal Ping Pong technique. That is that I will simply restate to Bill what I understood his feedback to be, clarify that I understood him correctly, and then pass the conversation on to someone else. So, I will say, "Bill, do I understand that you feel the biggest challenge that a home seller faces is that they are faced with paying too much commission to a real estate firm or selling their home on their own?" When he confirms that I understood his feedback I will say, "Thanks for that feedback, John, what is your opinion of what Bill said, do you have a similar opinion?"

Do you see how I hit the ball to Bill, he hit it back to me, and then I hit it to John? This is Verbal Ping Pong. I need to keep control of where the ball is and where it is going next. This will insure that everyone in the group is involved in the process and keep any one person from dominating the discussion. It is very important to continue this technique to insure that everyone who gives feedback feels as though you listened and understood their comments. After John gives his feedback I would say, "So I understand you correctly John, you feel that Bill is correct and that because there is no service developed to meet in the middle of doing it on your own and paying high commissions, sellers are forced to do it on their own. Did I understand you right?" After he confirms I will move on to the next person, "Sally, you heard both John and Bill, how do you feel about this issue?"

If you simply implement that strategy, you will have a very active and controlled discussion involving everyone in the room. The conversation will flow well and everyone will walk away feeling as though they contributed to your objectives and gave you the help that they had set out to give you. They will also feel as though their opinions were heard and valid. This is a critical component to these groups.

If you simply continue to use the Verbal Ping Pong method throughout the group, the discussion will flow from question to question. You will want to keep in mind the time constraints to insure that you move on to your follow up questions and get through the questions that you have for the group. The common mistake that many of the professionals that I work with make is that they get involved in the discussion and begin to run over on time. If this happens, the questionnaire will suffer and so will your results. It is important to stop the discussion to give adequate time for the questionnaire.

The Questionnaire

I always leave a minimum of ten minutes for the completion of the questionnaire. Even when the conversation is going very well with the group, I insure that I stop the group with ten minutes to go. I will say, "I appreciate the discussion that we are having and wish we could continue it. In the interest of sticking to the agenda, we need to move on to the questionnaire. I have allotted ten minutes to complete it so we should have plenty of time. I will leave the room to begin to prepare the food, please answer each question on there as thoroughly as you possibly can. That written feedback is going to very valuable to us."

I always leave the room for them to complete the questionnaire. If you do, they will quietly put their heads down and thoroughly answer the questions. If you stay in the room, they will ask questions, keep talking, and you will not get the answers to the questions that you need. Always have a reason to leave the room and tell them you will come back into the room in ten minutes. I will typically have food for focus group participants and will need to leave the room to get the food prepared.

The Food

While it seems simple, the food is actually a very important part of the focus group structure. When you complete the focus group, everyone will immediately leave unless they have a reason to stay. Even if they have additional comments or questions you will rarely hear them because they will assume the group is over and it is time to leave. That is why I have food for the participants. I will always have something very simple like sandwiches or pizza at the very end of the group. I also have "to go" boxes available for the participants who need to get going. I am aware that I have asked for one hour of their time and I have used that. The "to go" boxes are available for them to grab some food and get going if they need to.

For those who want to stick around and ask questions or give additional feedback, I tell them that they can certainly stick around and enjoy some food. This is the time that is great for interacting and building relationships with prospects, getting more feedback, or having prospects offer opportunities for your business in the form of referrals and introductions.

If you are using the Prospect Centered Focus Groups to introduce a new product or service and gain feedback, interested prospects will stick around and want to talk more about the product or service. Some will want to schedule time to discuss it further. This will typically all happen when the food is there. They will stay an additional half hour to an hour and converse together and with you. This is a sign that you have conducted an excellent group. When people want to stick around and talk rather than leave, they are showing you that they enjoyed the time.

At the conclusion of the group, you want to gather everybody's questionnaires and sincerely thank them for their participation. If they had questions or comments that require your follow up, insure them that you will contact them to follow up with a response. And then, relax, the hard part is over. Now you need to assess the groups' feedback, identify opportunities to improve and expand your business, and use the information available to you to continue to grow your business.

Step 8 – The Follow Up

I literally just got off of the phone with one of my clients. He said something that I think summarizes this process very well. He had done many workshops and public seminars over the years. He was tired of seeing his numbers go down and was convinced that workshops just don't work anymore. He did two focus groups with former workshop attendees to talk to them about their experience. He asked honest questions and said he had a group of prospects brainstorming with him for more than an hour.

The following night, he had an actual workshop. He told the workshop that he was going to try something different based on the feedback some of his focus groups told him and changed his presentation. In two back to back workshops, he increased his conversion more than 50% by implementing the simple suggestions of his focus groups. He paid me thousands to consult him, but I could have never told him what to change about that workshop. Only they could tell him that. Those two focus groups will be responsible for hundreds of thousands of dollars in revenue to his business.

While conducting Prospect Centered Focus Groups will naturally lead to new relationships with prospects and inevitably some focus group members will become clients—that cannot be your sole purpose for doing them. You have to understand that the gold is in the information and advice they give you. The gentleman mentioned above makes ten thousand dollars per client that he works with from the workshops. Would you rather have two of the participants in a focus group become clients or have the focus group teach you how to get four new clients a month for the rest of your career? This is the approach to take. Look at the feedback and the information that they give you as the real value to you. After the focus group, it is important to use the information to improve the business that you do. You will also receive information that allows you to help some of the people who attend the focus group. It is natural that they approach you if they have a need that you are able to help with. At no point should you make the group feel like that is the purpose. There are many ways to follow up with people who participate in your focus groups. The first is a letter that should go out to everyone and should be a combination of general comments about what you learned, and specific thanks for their specific feedback. An example of the banks letter is on the following page.

Dear John,

On behalf of ABC bank, I want to thank you for your participation in one of our focus groups. While we set out to learn some things about how to serve home sellers, I think we underestimated how much we would truly learn. I specifically appreciated your comments about using the bank as a trust builder but clarifying that the homes are not repossessions. That is helpful information and we have taken steps to change that.

Overall, we learned that our concept is on target and is designed to fill the void that exists in the market. We learned that we need to communicate that better in our marketing efforts. I also noted on your questionnaire that you felt it would be very valuable if we offered home valuations to home sellers. I will follow up with you on that and be happy to have one of our staff do that for you.

Overall, these focus groups were very helpful in our efforts to design a service that home sellers need and find valuable. I appreciated your willingness to participate and give us your time and your advice on accomplishing our objectives. Let us know if there is something that we can do to help you in your efforts beyond providing you a home valuation.

Respectfully,

Dan Allison
Vice President
ABC Bank

If you notice, the letter addresses several issues. Most importantly, it is a follow up to let the participant know that we did in fact complete a few focus groups and learned a great deal from doing so. It makes mention of their specific comments and contributions to the group so that they know that their specific participation was noticed and appreciated. It made mention of following up with them based on feedback they gave during the group and something that they would like to have done for them. Not only is it a courtesy to follow up on such a request, it is obviously very good for business. Finally, it lets them know that the bank will be there to help them when they need it.

This is just great for branding. A highly personalized approach to a very targeted prospect market. If you say you will follow up with them with information that was brought up in the focus group, insure that you follow up with them.

This brings up a very important issue. Don't ever call someone who participated in a focus group unless you specifically have a reason to. Respect their participation and send the letter only. You will see however that during or after the group, some participants bring up very specific issues that they need help with or information on. In this case, you don't need to hesitate to call them to offer them assistance. They will more than likely be grateful that you did and if you followed the steps outlined in this section, they will have a high level of respect for you and the way that you approach business.

I always use the questionnaires for future mailing campaigns. Rather than mass mail a bunch of random people a bunch of random things, I "rifle" market the people who attend my focus groups. They will share what their main issues are and what kinds of things they wish they better understood. I create a spreadsheet of people who have attended and what topics they find interesting based on their input in the focus group. Every couple of months, I use an internet search engine to find recent information on the topic and print it. I put a sticky note on it with a hand written note that may say, "Julie, I came across this the other day and thought it may help you." Whatever "it" is will be read because it is on a topic that is important to them. This takes very little time to do but can have a dramatic impact on building the relationship and having them view you as someone who wants to be of service. Imagine the impact to your business of having 75-100 of these people that you "rifle" market personalized material. They appreciate the information and you don't have to mass mail 5000 people who don't read what you send.

You have to insure that you are not just randomly following up with people who have participated in the focus groups. If you are presenting a product, service, strategy or process that is valuable to them, not only will they give you great feedback, but they will approach you about it. Think about it, if you had four focus groups compiled of 10 people per group you will have given a presentation of your offering and had discussions about it with 40 people. If none of those people take advantage of what you have, your questionnaires and discussion should tell you why it is not connecting with the audience. That alone is worth the $2000 you will spend to get in front of the 40 people. Changing your business based on their constructive feedback will earn you a great deal more than $2000 over just one year, much less your career.

If, however, you present something unique and valuable to the group of 40 people, not only will you receive great feedback and have excellent discussions, you will gain new clients in the process. None of which you had to sell. I don't believe that you can really sell anything to people. I think you need to educate people on what something is and what it can do for them and let them come to the conclusion that it will help them. Then, they will approach you.

In Conclusion – Prospect Centered Focus Groups

Many of you probably spend your time and resources marketing your unique products, services, processes and strategies to your target audience. Many of you are probably frustrated with the response that comes as a result of those marketing efforts. Prospect Centered Focus Groups are not a replacement for your marketing. They are a perfect compliment to it. If you do workshops and seminars to promote your services, every couple of months do a Prospect Centered Focus Group to come in and hear the workshop but give you honest feedback on its value and the offering. You will find that you can always learn from the people that you market to.

More importantly, you will find how willing people are to help you solve the problems that you may have. You will learn that one of the most powerful things that you can do in any marketing effort is hear the true feelings of the people you are trying to provide value to. As I always tell my clients, there is no silver bullet that works for every customer. Each potential customer holds a silver bullet in their hand. You need to politely ask for it and then ask them how they would prefer that you use it. Then, just do what they tell you.

IN CONCLUSION – FEEDBACK MARKETING

Feedback Marketing is the evolution of two simple concepts. Outbound marketing is designed to create awareness of your brand, your products, your services and the offerings that you have for the people that you want to serve. Surveys are an attempt to learn what the people that you serve feel about the products, services and offerings that you provide to them. Feedback Marketing allows you to accomplish both of those objectives simultaneously for a lot less money while having a lot more fun.

Whether you want to duplicate your top clients or be more valuable to your future clients, they have the answers to the questions you have. They know what is valuable and what their challenges are. They know what you need to do to become more referable. They know what you can improve to make their experience that much better. You simply need to have a platform to engage them in a conversation in a way that respects them as a customer, a potential customer, or a trusted relationship.

The power of Feedback Marketing creates a snowball effect. You can never look at one incident of any of the three strategies that we discussed in this book in isolation. While one group may not feel like it was beneficial, another can open unlimited opportunity. Feedback Marketing is not a destination; it is a way of doing business. It is a way of communicating your message to your target audience while giving them the respect and credibility that they deserve.

I will close by asking you a few questions:

If you spent 50 hours per year with your 50 best relationships talking about the direction your business is heading and then getting their feedback on how to accomplish your objectives and enlist their support; what impact would it have on your business one year from now?

If you spent 10 hours this year conducting 5 focus groups with your top 50 clients and relationships to educate them on the direction of your company and get their feedback on how to accomplish your objectives and enlist their support, what impact would that have on your business one year from now?

If you spent 10 hours this year conducting 5 focus groups with 50 ideal prospects to gain their insight into the value of your products and services and to understand how to provide the value they are looking for; what impact would that have on your business one year from now?

The three things that I just mentioned will cost you a grand total of $3000 this year and 70 hours of your life. They will get you in front of 100 top clients and relationships and 50 prospective clients. My final question to you is: Where will you be. . .one year from now?

Breinigsville, PA USA
15 September 2010
245416BV00004B/1/P